Speed, Agility and Quickness

for

WOMEN'S SOCCER

SAQ® Women's Soccer

Alan Pearson

A & C Black • London

Metric to Imperial conversions

1 centimetre (cm)	=	0.394 in
1 metre (m)	=	1.094 yd
1 kilometre (km)	=	1093.6 yd
1 kilogram (kg)	=	2.205 lb

First published 2003 by A&C Black Publishers Ltd
37 Soho Square, London W1D 3QZ
www.acblack.com

ISBN 0 7136 6377 4

A CIP catalogue record for this book is available from the British Library.

A&C Black uses paper produced with elemental chlorine-free pulp, harvested from managed sustainable forests.

Acknowledgements
Cover photograph courtesy of Empics; all other photographs courtesy of SAQ International; illustrations on pp. 121–3 by Dave Saunders; all others courtesy of Angus Nicol.

Typeset in Photina
Printed and bound in Great Britain by Biddles Ltd, Guildford and King's Lynn

Speed, Agility & Quickness International Limited Trade mark numbers:

'SAQ' ® Britain and Northern Ireland No. 2156613
'SAQ' ® European Community No. 001026277
'SAQ Speed, Agility, Quickness' ® Australia

SAQ ™

SAQ Programmes™
SAQ Equipment™
SAQ Training™
SAQ Accreditation Awards™

In addition to the above, the following trademarks are in current commercial use by SAQ International and have been for several years in respect to their products and services:

Fast Foot™ Ladder
Viper Belt™
SAQ Continuum™
Jelly Balls™
Micro Hurdles™
Macro Hurdles™
Speed Resistor™
Sprint Sled™
Power Harness™
Sonic Chute™
Agility Disc™
Side Strike®
Flexi-cord™
Velocity Builder™
Heel Lifter™
Visual Acuity Ring™
Peripheral Vision Stick™
Break Away Belt™ and Tri-Break Away Belt™
Dynamic Flex®
Bunt Bat™

The SAQ Continuum, SAQ Training, SAQ Programmes, SAQ Accreditation Awards and SAQ Equipment are products and services of Speed, Agility & Quickness International Limited (SAQ INTERNATIONAL) and its licensees. Only individual or corporate holders of valid SAQ Trainer certificates or valid SAQ Training licenses issued by SAQ INTER-NATIONAL may offer products or services under the SAQ brand name or logo (subject to terms).

Discover more about SAQ Programmes, SAQ Accreditation Awards and SAQ Equipment online at www.saqinternational.com

Contents

Acknowledgements iv

Forewords. v
Sue Lopez MBE
Hope Powell OBE

Introduction vi

1 Dynamic Flex
  warm–up on the move 1

2 Running form for soccer
  the mechanics of movement 34

3 Innervation
  fast feet, agility and control for
  soccer. 58

4 Accumulation of potential
  the SAQ Soccer Circuit. 74

5 Explosion
  3–step multi–directional acceleration
  for soccer 82

6 Expression of potential
  team games in preparation for the
  next level. 103

7 Position–specific drills. 110

8 Core stability development 138

9 Warm–down and recovery. 142

10 The SAQ Soccer Programme. 149

Glossary 162

References. 163

Index of drills 164

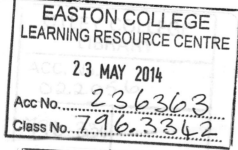

Acknowledgements

I would like to thank the Asfordby Amateurs Women's Football Club, especially Angie and Sharon for their support and assistance. The SAQ International staff have been a major driving force behind the development of our women's programme, especially Sarah Naylor, Angus Nicol, David Hawkins, Silvana Tiberio, Brian Benjamin and Mike Callow. Also thank you to Steve Palmer, Captain of Queens Park Rangers, for his insight into football.

A very special thank you to Sue Lopez who for years has constantly supported the women's game and the use of SAQ training principles.

Finally, love to my children James and Kira, and my fantastic wife Silvana, her sister Liliana and mum, Maria.

Alan Pearson
November 2002

Forewords

Speed and agility are key components of the physical profile of a successful soccer player, enabling players to cover ground efficiently and economically, as well as changing direction at high speed. 'SAQ Womens Soccer' covers a key physical aspect of training for soccer and presents information on warm-up and specific speed, agility and quickness exercises for soccer which has not previously been available to coaches. Exercises are well described and it is easy to perform the suggested training. The training is efficient and allows the players to develop key aspects of fitness and technical skills together. In the past, female players have been characterised as being technically skilful but physically slow and non-agile. The exercises outlined in this book, if followed in a safe, planned and progressive manner, will enable players to make huge improvements on those areas of fitness. This can only serve to further increase the performance of players and subsequently raise the profile of women's soccer. The book provides a wide variety of exercises and I would recommend it to anyone who wants to improve their performance in soccer.

Hope Powell OBE
Patron – Women's Sports Foundation

Hope Powell OBE is a former England international, having won 66 caps and scored 35 goals in a career that spanned from the age of 15 through to her retirement when she was appointed National Women's Coach at The FA in 1998. Powell made her debut at 11 years old for Millwall Lionesses and went on to win The FA Cup twice. As National Coach, she not only manages the Senior women's team but also oversees the Under-19s, Under-17s and Under-15s development pool. the National Player Development Centre at Loughborough as well as implementing a female coach mentoring scheme. She was awarded an OBE in the Queen's birthday honours in summer 2002.

SAQ Women's Soccer is an undoubted boost to the development of skilful female soccer players.

SAQ Training is ideally suited to refining girls' natural movements. They enjoy the opportunity to move dynamically and rhythmically, adapting their generally lighter and more fluid movements to a soccer context.

I certainly wish I could have trained 'the SAQ way' when I was playing for Southampton and England! As an FA 'A' Licence coach and SAQ Trainer I can at least coach players using these great techniques. My Physical Education teaching background convinces me that the SAQ Women's Soccer programme can enhance all movement for soccer, whatever the age and ability of the player.

Sue Lopez MBE
Head of Women's Soccer, Southampton FC
Director of Soccer, Southampton Saints
(Women's FA Premier League)

Sue Lopez MBE

■ Played 22 times for England

■ Winner FA Cup 8 times

■ FA Advanced Licence Coach, 1991

■ Founder and Director, FA Girls' Centre for Excellence, founded 1998

■ MBE for services to women's soccer, 2000

■ Sport England's Coach of the Year Award, 2000

■ Southampton FA Head of Women's Soccer, 2001

■ Scout for England's head coach

Introduction

THE FOUNDATION OF SAQ FOR WOMEN'S SOCCER

Soccer is one of the most played women's sports in the world. In the USA, in Europe, and particularly in the UK it has outgrown many sports more traditionally played by women. Who would have believed that not so long ago in England women were banned from playing this great game?

There is nothing more exhilarating than a soccer player who explodes through a defensive gap, checks, turns and sidesteps to avoid desperate defensive lunges and fires the ball home. Or when a centre half defies gravity by jumping into the air and hanging there long enough to intercept a crossed ball with her head before redirecting it to a supporting midfielder's feet for a swift decisive counter-attack. Soccer is the greatest game in the world.

These wonderful acts of speed, agility and quickness are what make the difference between winning and losing. Often thought to be God-given gifts and therefore neglected on the training field, they are admired and believed to be essential for success within the women's game by players, managers, coaches and trainers. Men no longer have the monopoly on athleticism, the gap between the sexes is decreasing all the time. Women can perform with exceptionally high levels of skill and physical ability.

The SAQ Programme for Soccer is the first-ever soccer-specific programme designed to develop these key skills. The programme also has other significant benefits such as improving eye, hand and foot co-ordination, strength, explosive power and core control, as well as being full of variety and great fun. The secret lies in the SAQ Continuum and the use of progressive sequential learning techniques, breaking down complex sports science and making

it easy to understand and practical to use. The end result is the development of multi-directional explosive speed specifically for soccer. This unique programme can be adapted to meet the needs of both squad training and individual players within a squad who require position-specific development. The Programme also provides an ideal opportunity for everyone, from children as young as 6 up to and including the most senior of professional players, to learn and improve.

The programme has evolved from a foundation of years of practical experience on the training fields of world soccer, talking to World Cup coaches, Premiership managers, elite and amateur players both male and female, through to the little league players and school kids. Many of Europe's top clubs now include SAQ Training as part of their everyday sessions because it adds a new dimension to their preparation and produces demonstrable results on the playing field.

This book enables coaches, trainers, managers and players to understand how and why SAQ Programmes work. It provides clear, precise examples of how to put the theory into practice on the training ground. Its progressive structure even covers advanced position-specific soccer drills that will allow SAQ Training to be integrated into all soccer training sessions.

What is SAQ Training?

Speed has long been considered as just a matter of how fast an object can go from point A to point B. Only recently has speed been studied and broken down into stages such as acceleration, the 'plaining out' phase, deceleration, etc. Much of this research has been carried out by sports coaches involved in straight-line running, so that the jumping, turning and zigzagging speed necessary in soccer has been somewhat neglected.

Those involved with the development of SAQ Programmes have sought to fill this void so as to develop all types of speed, particularly for team sports such as soccer. SAQ Programmes break speed down in to three main areas of skill: speed, agility and quickness. Although these may appear to be similar they are in fact quite different in terms of how they are trained, developed and integrated into a player's performance. When these skills are successfully combined and specialist SAQ Equipment is utilised, they provide the coach with the tools to make a good player into an outstanding one. It is remarkable what players can achieve with an SAQ Programme.

Speed

A crucial part of any player's game is the ability to cover the ground efficiently and economically over the first few yards and then to open up stride length and increase stride frequency when working over 40–50 yards. Speed means the maximum velocity a player can achieve and maintain. In most humans the ability to maintain this maximum velocity is for a short period of time and distance only. Speed can also be measured by the amount of time it takes a player to cover a particular distance.

Training to improve maximum speed requires a great deal of focus on correct running mechanics, stride length and frequency, the leg cycle and hip height/position. Drills such as the 'dead-leg run' and stride frequency drills that are used to help develop an economical running technique can all be easily integrated in a training session.

The best sprinters spend very little time in contact with the ground and what contact they do make is extremely efficient and powerful. Focusing on the mechanics of running helps to control and use this power efficiently and sparingly. Training when fresh is also crucial for an athlete/player to attain maximum speed. Many athletes can only reproduce top speeds for a few weeks of the year but the inclusion and practising of correct running mechanics on the training field will bring great benefit. How often have you seen a soccer player run as if they are also playing a kettledrum, that is, with poor arm mechanics? Such a running style will have a detrimental effect on the overall performance and, importantly, the speed of the player.

Agility

Agility is the ability to change direction without the loss of balance, strength, speed or body control. There is a direct link between improved agility and the development of an individual's timing, rhythm and movement.

Agility should not be taken for granted and can actually be taught to individual players. Training ensures that a soccer player develops the best offensive and defensive skills possible with the greatest quickness, speed and control and the least amount of wasted energy and movement. Agility also has many other benefits for the individual, helping to prevent niggling injuries and teaching the muscles how to fire properly and control minute shifts in ankle, knee, hip, back, shoulder and neck joints for the optimum body alignment.

Another very important benefit is that agility training is long-lasting. Unlike speed, stamina and weight training, it does not have to be maintained to retain the benefits. Consider the elderly person who can still ride a bicycle 40 years after having last ridden one. Agility training acts like an indelible mark, programming muscle memory.

THE FOUR ELEMENTS OF AGILITY

There are four elements to agility:

- balance
- co-ordination
- programmed agility and
- random agility

Within these there is speed, strength, timing and rhythm.

Balance is a foundation of athleticism. Here we teach the ability to stand, stop and walk by focusing on the centre of gravity; balance can be taught and retained relatively quickly. Examples include: standing on one leg, walking on a balance beam, standing on a balance beam, standing on an agility disc, walking backwards with your eyes closed and jumping on a mini trampoline and then freezing. It does not take too long to train balance. It requires only a couple of minutes, two or three times a week and should be done early in the morning and early in a training session.

Balance is complicated with additional stresses. **Co-ordination** is the goal of mastering simple skills under more difficult stresses. Co-ordination work is often slow and methodical with an emphasis on correct biomechanics during athletically demanding movements. Training co-ordination can be completed by breaking a skill down into sections then gradually bringing them together. Co-ordination activities include footwork drills, tumbling, rolling and jumping. More difficult examples are walking on a balance beam while playing catch, running along a line while a partner lightly pulls and pushes in an attempt to move the player off the line and jumping on and off an agility disc while holding a jelly ball.

The third element of agility training is called **programmed agility**. This involves a player who has already experienced the skill or stress that is to be placed on him/her and is aware of the pattern and sequence of demands of that experience. In short, the player has already been programmed. Programmed agility drills can be conducted at high speeds but must be learnt at low, controlled speeds. Examples are zigzag cone drills, shuttle runs and T cone drills, all of which involve change of direction along a known standardised pattern. There is no spontaneity.

Once these types of drills are learnt and performed on a regular basis, times and performances will improve and advances in strength, explosion, flexibility and body control will be witnessed. This is true of players of any ability.

The final element, the most difficult to master, prepare for and perform is **random agility**. Here the player performs tasks with unknown patterns and unknown demands. Here the coach can incorporate visual and audible reactive skills so that the player has to make split-second decisions with movements based upon the various stimuli. The skill level is now becoming much closer to actual game situations. Random agility can be trained by games such as tag, read and react (tennis ball drops and dodge), dodge ball and more specific training such as jumping and landing followed by an immediate unexpected movement demand from the coach.

Agility training is challenging, fun and exciting. There is the opportunity for tremendous variety and training should not become boring or laborious. Agility is not just for those with elite sporting abilities – try navigating through a busy shopping mall.

Quickness

When a player accelerates a great deal of force has to be generated and transferred through the foot to the ground. This action is similar to that of rolling a towel up (the 'leg'), holding one end in your hand and flicking it out to achieve a cracking noise from the other end (the 'foot'). The act of acceleration in a fraction of a second takes the body from a static position to motion. Muscles actually lengthen and then shorten instantaneously – that is an 'eccentric' followed by a 'concentric' contraction. This process is known as the stretch shortening cycle action (SCC). SAQ Training concentrates on improving the neuro-muscular system that impacts on this process, so that this initial movement – whether lateral, linear or vertical – is automatic, explosive and precise. The reaction time is the time it takes for the brain to receive and respond to a stimulus by sending a message to the muscle causing it to contract. This is what helps a soccer player to cut right – left – right again and then burn down the sideline, or the goalkeeper to make a split-second reaction save. With ongoing SAQ Training, the neuro-muscular system is reprogrammed and restrictive mental blocks and thresholds are removed. Consequently messages from the brain have a clear path to the muscles, and the result is an instinctively quicker player.

Quickness training begins with 'innervation' (isolated fast contractions of an individual joint). For example, repeating the same explosive movement over a short period of time, such as fast feet and line drills. These quick repetitive motions take the body through the gears moving it in a co-ordinated manner to develop speed. Integrating quickness training throughout the year by using fast feet and reaction-type drills will result in the muscles having increased firing rates. This means that players are capable of faster, more controlled acceleration. The goal is to ensure that your players explode over the first 3–5 yards. Imagine that the firing between the nervous system and the muscles are the gears in a car, the timing, speed and smoothness of the gear change means the wheels and thus the car accelerate away efficiently, with balance and co-ordination so that the wheels do not spin and the car does not lose control.

Movement skills

Many elements of balance and co-ordination involve the processing of sensory information from within the body. Proprioceptors are sensors that detect muscular tension, tension in tendons, relative tension and pressure in the skin. In addition, the body has a range of other sensors that detect balance. The ability to express balance and co-ordination is highly dependent on the effectiveness of the body's internal sensors and proprioceptors, just like the suspension on a car. Through training, these sensors, and the neural communication system within the body, become more effective. In addition, the brain becomes more able to interpret these messages and formulate the appropriate movement response. This physiological development underpins effective movement and future movement skill development.

SAQ Equipment

SAQ Equipment adds variety and stimulus to your training session. Drill variations are unlimited and once mastered, the results achieved can be quite astonishing. Players of all ages and abilities enjoy the challenges presented to them when training with SAQ Equipment, particularly when introduced in a soccer-specific manner.

When using SAQ Equipment, coaches, trainers and players must be aware of the safety issues involved and of the reduced effectiveness and potentially dangerous consequence of using inappropriate or inferior equipment.

The following pages introduce a variety of SAQ Equipment recommended for use in many of the drills detailed later in this book.

FAST FOOT LADDERS

These are made of webbing with round, hard plastic rungs spaced approx. 18 inches apart; they come in sets of two pieces each measuring 15 feet. The pieces can be joined together or used as two separate ladders; they can also be folded over to create different angles for players to perform drills on. Fast Foot Ladders are great for improving agility and for the development of explosive fast feet.

MICRO & MACRO V HURDLES

These come in two sizes; Micro V Hurdles measuring 7 inches and Macro V Hurdles measuring 12 inches in height. They are constructed of a hard plastic and have been specifically designed as a safe freestanding piece of equipment. It is recommended that the hurdles be used in sets of 6–8 to perform the mechanics drills detailed later. They are ideal for practising running mechanics and low-impact plyometrics. The Micro V Hurdles are also great for lateral work.

SONIC CHUTE

These are made from webbing (the belt), nylon cord and a lightweight cloth 'chute', the size of which may vary from 5 to 6 foot. The belt has a release mechanism that, when pulled, drops the chute so that the player can explode forwards. Sonic chutes are great for developing sprint endurance.

VIPER BELT

This is a resistance belt specially made for high-intensity training. It has three stainless steel anchor points where a flexi-cord can be attached. The flexi-cord is made from surgical tubing with a specific elongation. The Viper Belt has a safety belt and safety fasteners; it is double stitched and provides a good level of resistance. This piece of equipment is useful for developing explosive speed in all directions.

SIDE-STEPPERS

These are padded ankle straps that are connected together by an adjustable flexi-cord. They are useful for the development of lateral movements.

REACTOR

A rubber ball specifically shaped so that it bounces in unpredictable directions.

OVERSPEED TOW ROPE

This is made up of two belts and a 50-yard nylon cord pulley system. It can be used to provide resistance and is specifically designed for the development of express overspeed and swerve running.

BREAK-AWAY BELT

This is a webbing belt that is connected by Velcro-covered connecting strips. It is good for mirror drills and position-specific marking drills, breaking apart when one player gets away from the other.

STRIDE FREQUENCY CANES

Plastic, 4-foot canes of different colours that are used to mark out stride patterns.

SPRINT SLED

A metal sled with a centre area to accommodate different weights and a running harness that is attached by webbing straps of 8–10 yards in length.

JELLY BALLS

Round, soft rubber balls filled with a water-based jelly-like substance. They come in different weights from 4 to 18 lb. They differ from the old-fashioned medicine balls because they can be bounced with great force on to hard surfaces.

HAND WEIGHTS

Foam-covered weights of 1.5–2.5 lb. They are safe and easy to use both indoors and out.

VISUAL ACUITY RING

A hard plastic ring of approx 30 inches in diameter with four different coloured balls attached to it, all equally distributed around the ring. The ring helps to develop visual acuity and tracking skills when thrown and caught between the players. This piece of equipment is particularly good for goalkeepers.

PERIPHERAL VISION STICK

The stick is simple but very effective for the training of peripheral vision. It is approximately 4 feet long with a brightly coloured ball at one end. Once again this is effective for all players and particularly for goalkeepers.

BUNT BAT

A 4-foot stick with three coloured balls – one at each end and one in the middle. Working in pairs, player 1 holds the bat with two hands while player 2 throws a small ball or bean bag for player 1 to 'bunt' or fend off. This is effective for all players but particularly so for goalkeepers' hand–eye co-ordination.

AGILITY DISC

An inflatable rubber disc 18 inches across. The discs are multi-purpose but particularly good for proprioceptive and core development work (to strengthen the deep muscles of the trunk). They can be stood on, knelt on, sat on and lain on for the performance of all types of exercises.

The SAQ Continuum

Many games activities are characterised by explosive movements, acceleration and deceleration, agility, turning ability and speed of responses (Smythe 2000). The SAQ Continuum is the sequence and progression of components that make up a SAQ Training session. The progressive elements include soccer-specific patterns of running and drills including ball work. The Continuum is also flexible and once the pre-season foundation work has been completed, during the season when time and recovery are of the essence short combination SAQ Training sessions provide a constant top-up to the skills that have already been learned.

SAQ Training is like any other fitness training – if neglected then players' explosive multi-directional power will diminish. The component parts of the SAQ Continuum and how they relate to soccer are:

- **Dynamic Flex** – warm-up on the move
- **mechanics of movement** – the development of running form for soccer
- **innervation** – fast feet, agility and control for soccer
- **accumulation of potential** – the bringing together of the previous components in a SAQ Training soccer circuit
- **explosion** – the development of explosive 3-step multi-directional acceleration for soccer
- **expression of potential** – short competitive team games that prepare the players for the next level of training
- **warm-down**

Throughout the continuum, position-specific drills and skills can be implemented.

WARM-UP ON THE MOVE

It is common knowledge that before engaging in intense or strenuous exercise the body should be prepared. The warm-up should achieve a change in a number of physiological responses in order that the body can work safely and effectively:

- increased body temperature, specifically core (deep) muscle temperature
- increased heart rate and blood flow
- increased breathing rate
- increased elasticity of muscular tissues
- activated neuro-muscular system
- increased mental alertness.

The warm-up should take a performer from a rested state, to the physiological state required for participation in the session that is to follow. The warm-up should gradually increase in intensity as the session goes on. In addition it should be fun and stimulating for the players, switching them on mentally.

What is Dynamic Flex?

The standard training session for soccer begins by warming the players up before taking them through a series of stretches that focus on the main muscle groups in the body. However, 'static' stretches like this are not really relevant within a game of soccer. Players do not need to be able to do the splits like gymnasts and dancers, but they do need to be able to perform an overhead kick or a side-on volley. Dynamic Flex is what allows a soccer player to do this: flexibility in action, if you like, combined with power and strength.

Indeed, the most recent research has shown that static stretching before training or competition can actually be detrimental to performance. One study found that the eccentric strength of the muscle – its strength when lengthening, for instance when a soccer player brakes or lands from a jump – was reduced by 7–9% for up to an hour after static stretching. Similarly, it was discovered that there was a clear decrease in the peak power output of the muscle after stretching.

Dynamic stretching, however, has been shown to increase muscle warmth and, therefore, elasticity. This is vital for performance and muscle safety. Indeed, one of the main arguments in favour of static stretching – that it helps to prevent injury – has also now been called into question. Recent research suggests that static stretching has almost no effect on this (Gleim and McHugh 1997). Similarly, an Australian Army physiotherapist (Pope 1999) studied army recruits over the course of a year. He instructed half to warm up with static stretching, and half to warm up without any stretching at all. He found no differences in the incidence of injury between the two groups, suggesting that static stretching is of little benefit in the pre-exercise warm-up.

The Warm-up

Using a standard 20 × 20 yard grid (*see* fig. 1.1). The following exercises represent a foundation set of Dynamic Flex™ warm-up drills. Also included in this chapter are variations and the introduction of the ball.

It is important to remember that soccer players not only enjoy variety but also that they respond proactively on the field to the variations in training. Once they have mastered the standard set the introduction of new grids (*see* figs. 1.2–6) and combination work including the ball will ensure maximum participation.

In a warm-up drill, start slowly, rehearse the movements then increase the intensity.

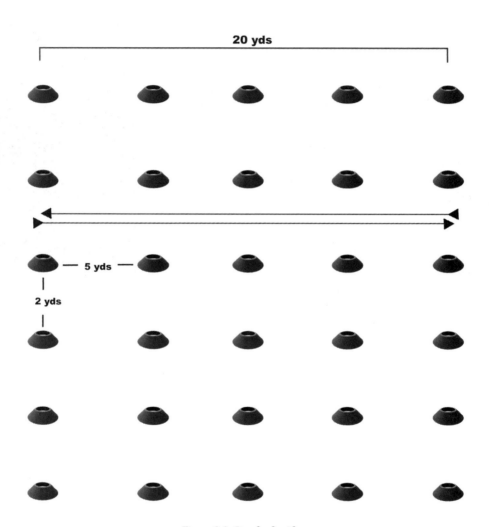

Figure 1.1 Standard grid

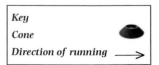

Key
Cone
Direction of running ⟶

DRILL WALKING ON THE BALLS OF THE FEET

Aim
To stretch shins and improve ankle mobility. To improve balance and co-ordination. To increase body temperature.

Area/equipment
An indoor or outdoor grid 20 yards in length. The width of the grid is variable depending on the size of the squad.

Description
Player to cover the length of the grid by walking on the balls of the feet. Return to the start by repeating the drill in a backward motion.

Key teaching points
- Do not walk on the toes
- Keep off the heels
- Maintain correct arm mechanics (*see* page 34)
- Maintain an upright posture

Sets and reps
2×20 yards, 1 forwards and 1 backwards.

Variations/progressions
Perform the drill laterally but do not allow the feet to come together completely. Push off with the back foot, do not pull with the lead foot.

DRILL ANKLE FLICKS

Aim
To stretch calves and improve ankle mobility. To improve balance, co-ordination and rhythm of movement. To prepare for good foot/floor contact. To increase body temperature.

Area/equipment
An indoor or outdoor grid 20 yards in length. The width of the grid is variable depending on the size of the squad.

Description
Player to cover the length of the grid in a skipping motion where the balls of the feet plant then flick up towards the shin. The player should be seen to move in a bouncing manner. Return to the start by repeating the drill in a backward motion.

Key teaching points
- Work off the balls of the feet, not the toes
- Practise the first few steps on the spot before moving off
- Maintain correct arm mechanics (*see* page 34)
- Maintain an upright posture

Sets and reps
2 × 20 yards, 1 forwards and 1 backwards.

Variations/progressions
Perform the drill laterally.

DRILL SMALL SKIPS

Aim
To improve lower leg flexibility and ankle mobility. To improve balance, co-ordination and rhythm and to develop positive foot/ground contact. To increase body temperature.

Area/equipment
An indoor or outdoor grid 20 yards in length. The width of the grid is variable depending on the size of the squad.

Description
Player to cover the length of the grid in a low skipping motion. Return to the start by repeating the drill in a backward motion.

Key teaching points
- Raise knee to an angle of about 45–55°
- Work off the ball of the foot
- Maintain correct arm mechanics (*see* page 34)
- Maintain an upright posture
- Maintain a good rhythm

Sets and reps
2 × 20 yards, 1 forwards and 1 backwards.

Variations/progressions
Perform the drill laterally.

DRILL | *WIDE SKIP*

Aim
To improve hip and ankle mobility. To improve balance, co-ordination and rhythm. To increase body temperature.

Area/equipment
An indoor or outdoor grid 20 yards in length. The width of the grid is variable depending on the size of the squad.

Description
Player to cover the length of the grid by skipping. The feet should remain shoulder-width apart and the knees face outwards at all times. Return to the start by repeating the drill in a backward motion.

Key teaching points
- Keep off the heels
- Maintain correct arm mechanics (*see* page 34)
- Maintain an upright posture
- Do not take the thigh above a 90° angle

Sets and reps
2 × 20 yards, 1 forwards and 1 backwards.

Variations/progressions
Perform the drill laterally.

DRILL KNEE OUT SKIP

Aim
To stretch the inner thigh and improve hip mobility. To develop an angled knee drive, balance, co-ordination and rhythm. To increase body temperature.

Area/equipment
An indoor or outdoor grid 20 yards in length. The width of the grid is variable depending on the size of the squad.

Description
Player to cover the length of the grid in a skipping motion. The knee moves from the centre of the body to a position outside the body before returning to the central position. Return to the start by repeating the drill in a backward motion.

Key teaching points
■ Feet start in a linear position and move outwards as the knee is raised
■ Work off the balls of the feet
■ The knee is to be pushed, not rolled, out and back
■ Maintain correct arm mechanics (*see* page 34)
■ The movement should be smooth, not jerky

Sets and reps
2 × 20 yards, 1 forwards and 1 backwards.

Variations/progressions
Perform the drill laterally.

DRILL   *SINGLE-KNEE DEAD-LEG LIFT*

Aim
To improve buttock flexibility and hip mobility. To isolate the correct 'running cycle' motion for each leg.

Area/equipment
An indoor or outdoor grid 20 yards in length. The width of the grid is variable depending on the size of the squad.

Description
Player to cover the length of the grid by bringing the knee of one leg quickly up to a 90° position. The other leg should remain as straight as possible with a very short lift away from the ground throughout the movement. The ratio should be 1:4, i.e. 1 lift to every 4 steps. Work one leg on the way down the grid and the other on the return.

Key teaching points
■ Do not raise knees above 90°
■ Strike the floor with the ball of the foot
■ Keep the foot in a linear position
■ Maintain correct running mechanics (*see* page 34)

Sets and reps
2 × 20 yards, 1 forwards and 1 backwards.

Variations/progressions
Vary the lift ratio, e.g. 1:2.

Side view

DRILL *HIGH KNEE-LIFT SKIP*

Aim
To improve buttock flexibility and hip mobility. To increase the range of motion (ROM) over a period of time. To develop rhythm. To increase body temperature.

Area/equipment
An indoor or outdoor grid 20 yards in length. The width of the grid is variable depending on the size of the squad.

Description
Player to cover the length of the grid in a high skipping motion. Return to the start by repeating the drill in a backward motion.

Key teaching points
- Thigh to be taken past 90°
- Work off the balls of the feet
- Maintain a strong core
- Maintain an upright posture
- Control the head by looking forwards at all times
- Maintain correct arm mechanics (*see* page 34)

Sets and reps
2 × 20 yards, 1 forwards and 1 backwards.

Variations/progressions
Perform the drill laterally.

DRILL KNEE-ACROSS SKIP

Aim
To improve outer hip flexibility and hip mobility over a period of time. To develop balance and co-ordination. To increase body temperature.

Area/equipment
An indoor or outdoor grid 20 yards in length. The width of the grid is variable depending on the size of the squad.

Description
Player to cover the length of the grid in a skipping motion where the knee comes across the body. Return to the start by repeating the drill in a backward motion.

Key teaching points
- Do not force an increased ROM
- Work off the balls of the feet
- Maintain a strong core
- Maintain an upright posture
- Control the head by looking forward at all times
- Use the arms primarily for balance

Sets and reps
2 × 20 yards, 1 forwards and 1 backwards.

Variations/progressions
Perform the drill laterally.

DRILL LATERAL RUNNING

Aim
To develop economic knee drive, stretch the side of the quadriceps and prepare for an efficient lateral running technique. To increase body temperature.

Area/equipment
An indoor or outdoor grid 20 yards in length. The width of the grid is variable depending on the size of the squad.

Description
Player to cover the length of the grid with the left or right shoulder leading, taking short lateral steps. Return with the opposite shoulder leading.

Key teaching points
- Keep the hips square
- Work off the balls of the feet
- Do not skip
- Do not let the feet cross over
- Maintain an upright posture
- Do not sink into the hips (*see* page 34) or fold at the waist
- Do not overstride – use short, sharp steps
- Maintain correct arm mechanics (*see* page 34)

Sets and reps
2 × 20 yards, 1 leading with the left shoulder and 1 with the right.

Variations/progressions
Practise lateral-angled zigzag runs.

DRILL PRE-TURN

Aim
To prepare the hips for a turning action without committing the whole body. To increase body temperature and improve body control.

Area/equipment
An indoor or outdoor grid 20 yards in length. The width of the grid is variable depending on the size of the squad.

Description
Player to cover the length of the grid by performing a lateral movement. The heel of the back foot is moved to a position almost alongside the lead foot. Just before the feet come together, the lead foot is moved away laterally. Return to the start by repeating the drill but lead with the opposite shoulder.

Key teaching points
- The back foot must not cross the lead foot
- Work off the balls of the feet
- Maintain correct arm mechanics (*see* page 34)
- Maintain an upright posture
- Do not sink into the hips (*see* page 34) or fold at the waist
- Do not use a high knee-lift; the angle should be no more than 45°

Sets and reps
2 × 20 yards, 1 leading with the left shoulder and 1 with the right.

DRILL   *CARIOCA*

Aim
To improve hip mobility and speed, which will increase the firing of nerve impulses over a period of time. To develop balance and co-ordination whilst moving and twisting. To increase body temperature.

Area/equipment
An indoor or outdoor grid 20 yards in length. The width of the grid is variable depending on the size of the squad.

Description
Player to cover the length of the grid by moving laterally. The rear foot crosses in front of the body and then moves around to the back. Simultaneously, the lead foot does the opposite. The arms also move across the front and back of the body.

Key teaching points
- Start slowly and build up the tempo
- Work off the balls of the feet
- Keep the shoulders square
- Do not force the ROM
- Use the arms primarily for balance

Sets and reps
2 × 20 yards, 1 leading with the left leg and 1 with the right.

Variations/progressions
Perform the drill laterally with a partner (mirror drills) i.e. one initiates/leads the movement while the other attempts to follow.

DRILL *SIDE LUNGE*

Aim
To stretch the inner thighs and gluteals (buttocks). To develop balance and co-ordination. To increase body temperature.

Area/equipment
An indoor or outdoor grid 20 yards in length. The width of the grid is variable depending on the size of the squad.

Description
Player to cover the length of the grid by performing lateral lunges. Take a wide lateral step and simultaneously lower the gluteals towards the ground. Return to the start with the opposite shoulder leading.

Key teaching points
- Do not bend at the waist or lean forward
- Try to keep off the heels
- Maintain a strong core and keep upright
- Use the arms primarily for balance

Sets and reps
2 × 20 yards, 1 leading with the left shoulder and 1 with the right.

Variations/progressions
Work in pairs facing each other and chest-passing the ball.

DRILL *HAMSTRING BUTTOCK FLICKS*

Aim
To stretch the front and back of thighs and improve hip mobility. To increase body temperature.

Area/equipment
An indoor or outdoor grid 20 yards in length. The width of the grid is variable depending on the size of the squad.

Description
Player to cover the length of the grid by moving forwards alternating leg flicks where the heel moves up towards the buttocks. On the return to the start repeat the drill but work backwards.

Key teaching points
- Start slowly and build up the tempo
- Work off the balls of the feet
- Maintain an upright posture
- Do not sink into the hips
- Try to develop a rhythm

Sets and reps
2×20 yards, 1 forwards and 1 backwards.

Variations/progressions
- Perform the drill laterally
- Perform the drill as above but flick the heel to the outside of the buttocks

DRILL HEEL TO INSIDE OF THIGH SKIP

Aim
To stretch the hamstrings, groin and gluteals. To improve balance and co-ordination and to increase body temperature.

Area/equipment
An indoor or outdoor grid 20 yards in length. The width of the grid is variable depending on the size of the squad.

Description
Player to cover the length of the grid in a skipping motion where the heel of one leg comes up almost to touch the inside thigh of the opposite leg. Imagine there is a football on a piece of string that is hanging centrally just below your waist and you are trying to kick it with alternate heels. Return backwards.

Key teaching points
- Start slowly and build up the tempo
- Work off the balls of the feet
- Maintain an upright posture
- Maintain a strong core throughout
- Use arms for balance

Sets and reps
2 × 20 yards, 1 forwards and 1 backwards.

Variations/progressions
Perform the drill laterally.

DRILL *SIDEWAYS HEEL FLICKS*

Aim
To stretch gluteals, outer hamstrings and outer thighs. To develop rhythm and co-ordination and to increase body temperature.

Area/equipment
An indoor or outdoor grid 20 yards in length. The width of the grid is variable depending on the size of the squad.

Description
Player to cover the length of the grid by performing a skipping motion where the heel is flicked up and out to the side. Complete the grid performing the drill on alternate legs before repeating backwards.

Key teaching points
- Start slowly and build up the tempo
- Work off the balls of the feet
- Maintain an upright posture and strong core
- Use arms for balance
- Try to develop a rhythm

Sets and reps
2 × 20 yards, 1 forwards and 1 backwards.

Variations/progressions
Perform the drill laterally.

DRILL HURDLE WALK

Aim
To stretch inner and outer thighs and to increase ROM. To develop balance and co-ordination and increase body temperature.

Area/equipment
An indoor or outdoor grid 20 yards in length. The width of the grid is variable depending on the size of the squad.

Description
Player to cover the length of the grid by walking in a straight line and lifting alternate legs as if going over high hurdles. On the return to the start repeat the drill but travel backwards.

Key teaching points
- Try to keep the body square as the hips rotate
- Work off the balls of the feet
- Maintain an upright posture
- Do not sink into the hips or bend over at the waist
- Imagine that you are actually stepping over a barrier

Sets and reps
2 × 20 yards, 1 forwards and 1 backwards.

DRILL   *RUSSIAN WALK*

Aim
To stretch the back of the thighs. To improve hip mobility and ankle stabilisation. To develop balance and co-ordination and increase body temperature.

Area/equipment
An indoor or outdoor grid 20 yards in length. The width of the grid is variable depending on the size of the squad.

Description
Player to cover the length of the grid by performing a walking march with a high extended step. Imagine that the aim is to scrape the sole of your shoe down the front of a door. Return to the start by repeating the drill in a backward motion.

Key teaching points
■ Lift the knee before extending the leg
■ Work off the balls of the feet
■ Try to keep off the heels, particularly on the back foot
■ Keep the hips square

Sets and reps
2 × 20 yards, both forwards.

Variations/progressions
Perform the drill backwards.

DRILL WALKING LUNGE

Aim
To stretch the front of hips and thighs. To develop balance and co-ordination and increase body temperature.

Area/equipment
An indoor or outdoor grid 20 yards in length. The width of the grid is variable depending on the size of the squad.

Description
Player to cover the length of the grid by performing a walking lunge. The front leg should be bent with a 90° angle at the knee and the thigh in a horizontal position. The back leg should also be at a 90° angle but with the knee touching the ground and the thigh in a vertical position. Return to the start by repeating the drill in a backward motion.

Key teaching points
- Try to keep the hips square
- Maintain a strong core and keep upright
- Maintain good control
- Persevere with backward lunges – these are difficult to master

Sets and reps
2 × 20 yards, 1 forwards and 1 backwards.

Variations/progressions
- Perform the drill with hand weights
- Perform the drill while catching and passing a ball in the down position

DRILL *WALKING HAMSTRING*

Aim
To stretch the backs of the thighs.

Area/equipment
An indoor or outdoor grid 20 yards in length. The width of the grid is variable depending on the size of the squad.

Description
Player to cover the length of the grid by extending the lead leg heel first onto the ground and rolling onto the ball of the foot. Walk forwards and repeat on the opposite leg, continue in this manner alternating the lead leg. For comfort, cross arms.

Key teaching points
- Keep the spine straight
- Do not bend over
- Control the head by looking forwards at all times
- Work at a steady pace, do not rush

Sets and reps
2 × 20 yards, 1 forwards and 1 backwards.

DRILL WALL DRILL – LEG OUT AND ACROSS BODY

Aim
To increase the ROM in the hip region. To increase body temperature.

Area/equipment
A wall or fence to lean against.

Description
The player faces and leans against the wall/fence at a 20–30° angle, and swings the leg across the body from one side to the other. Repeat on the other leg.

Key teaching points
- Do not force an increased ROM
- Work off the ball of the support foot
- Lean with both hands against the wall/fence
- Keep the hips square
- Do not look down
- Gradually speed up the speed of the movement

Sets and reps
7–10 on each leg.

Variations/progressions
Lean against a partner.

DRILL *WALL DRILL – LINEAR LEG FORWARD/BACK*

Aim
To increase the ROM in the hip region. To increase body temperature.

Area/equipment
A wall or fence to lean against.

Description
The player faces and leans against the wall/fence at an angle of 20–30°, takes the leg back and swings it forward in a linear motion along the same plane. Repeat with the other leg.

Key teaching points
- Do not force an increased ROM
- Work off the ball of the support foot
- Lean with both hands against the wall/fence
- Do not look down
- Gradually increase speed

Sets and reps
7–10 on each leg.

Variations/progressions
Lean against a partner.

DRILL — *WALL DRILL – KNEE ACROSS BODY*

Aim
To increase the ROM in the hip region. To increase body temperature.

Area/equipment
A wall or fence to lean against.

Description
The player faces and leans against the wall/fence at an angle of 20–30°, and from a standing position, drives one knee upwards and across the body. Repeat with the other leg.

Key teaching points
- Do not force an increased ROM
- Work off the ball of the support foot
- Lean with both hands against the wall/fence
- Keep the hips square
- Do not look down
- Gradually increase speed
- Imagine you are trying to get your knee up and across your body to the opposite pocket

Sets and reps
7–10 on each leg.

Variations/progressions
Lean against a partner.

DRILL *PAIR DRILL – LATERAL RUNS*

Aim

To develop running skills in a more game-specific situation. To stimulate balance and co-ordination and to practise reassertion of the correct mechanics. To increase body temperature.

Area/equipment

An indoor or outdoor grid 20 yards in length. The width of the grid is variable depending on the size of the squad.

Description

Refer to lateral running drill (*see* page 11). The players face each other 2–3 feet apart and cover the length of the grid sideways, taking short lateral steps. Occasionally they can push each other.

Key teaching points

- Refer to lateral running drills (*see* page 11)
- When off balance or after being pushed, the focus should be on the reassertion of the correct arm and foot mechanics

Sets and reps

2 × 20 yards, 1 leading with the left leg and 1 with the right.

Variations/progressions

Introduce the ball and pass hand to hand and then hand to foot.

DRILL PAIR DRILL – JOCKEYING

Aim
To simulate defensive and attacking close-quarter movement patterns. To increase body temperature.

Area/equipment
An indoor or outdoor grid 20 yards in length. The width of the grid is variable depending on the size of the squad.

Description
Players to stand facing each other and to cover the grid working both forwards and backwards. The player moving forwards (attacker) will show first the left and then the right shoulder alternately in a rhythmic motion. The player moving backwards (defender) mirrors the attacking player's movements.

Key teaching points
- Take short steps
- Do not cross the feet
- Maintain a strong core and an upright posture
- Do not sink into the hips
- Keep your eyes on the opponent at all times

Sets and reps
2 × 20 yards, 1 leading with the left leg and 1 with the right.

Variations/progressions
Introduce the ball to the attacking player who presses with the ball at her feet, transferring it from left to right to keep the defender on her toes.

DRILL FORWARD/BACKWARD RUN WITH CONTACT

Aim

To simulate physical contact while faced directly with a close-marking opponent. To develop reassertion of balance, co-ordination and agility and to increase body temperature.

Area/equipment

An indoor or outdoor grid 20 yards in length. The width of the grid is variable depending on the size of the squad.

Description

The players face each other about 1 yard apart. One player runs forwards while the other faces her and runs backwards, occasionally they lightly push each other. The drill should be repeated with the roles reversed.

Key teaching points

- Do not sink into the hips
- When off balance or after being pushed, the focus should be on the reassertion of the correct arm and foot mechanics
- Work hard to maintain a strong core throughout the drill

Sets and reps

2 × 20 yards, 1 forwards and 1 backwards.

Variations/progressions

Perform the drill with both players facing the same direction and therefore one of the players being pushed from behind.

DRILL   PAIR DRILL – SIDE BY SIDE CONTACT RUN

Aim
To simulate physical contact while running during a game. To develop reassertion of balance, co-ordination and agility when closely challenged and to increase body temperature.

Area/equipment
An indoor or outdoor grid 20 yards in length. The width of the grid is variable depending on the size of the squad.

Description
Players stand side by side and cover the grid running linearly and occasionally contacting each other with their shoulders. The drill should be repeated with the players using the opposite shoulders.

Key teaching points
- Practise the use of peripheral vision instead of turning the head
- When off balance or after being pushed, the focus should be on the reassertion of the correct arm and foot mechanics
- Work hard to maintain a strong core throughout

Sets and reps
2 × 20 yards, 1 contacting with the left shoulder and 1 with the right.

Variations/progressions
Perform the drill with one player holding her partner off for the entire length of the grid.

DRILL   *SELECTION OF SPRINTS*

Aim
To increase the intensity of the warm-up and prepare players for maximum exertion. To speed up the firing rate of neuro-muscular messages. To increase body temperature.

Area/equipment
An indoor or outdoor grid 20 yards in length. The width of the grid is variable depending on the size of the squad. Sprint one way only, perform a jog-back recovery on the outside of the grid.

Description
Players to start from different angles – e.g. side-on, backwards, etc. – and to accelerate into a forward running motion down the grid.

Key teaching points
- Maintain good running mechanics (*see* page 34)
- Ensure that players alternate the lead foot

Sets and reps
1 set of 5 sprints, varying the start position.

Variations/progressions
- Include swerving sprints
- Include turns in the sprints

DRILL GRID VARIATIONS

Aim

To stimulate and motivate players with a variety of movement patterns.

Area/equipment

Mark out an indoor or outdoor grid 20 yards in length with cones placed at 5-yard intervals. The width of the grid is variable depending on the size of the squad. Place a line of cones on each side of the grid about 2 yards away with 1 yard between each cone.

Description

Perform Dynamic Flex down the grid with the group splitting around the end cones to return on the outside of the grid. On reaching the cones the players should zigzag back through them.

Key teaching points

The timing is critical – players should be constantly on the move.

Sets and reps

Players can perform the entire Dynamic Flex warm-up in this manner.

Variations/progressions

Replace the cones on the outside of the grid with Fast Foot ladders or hurdles.

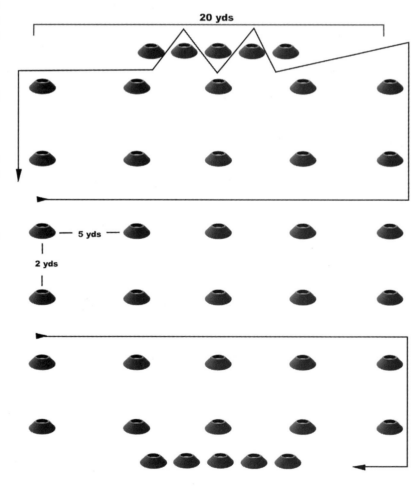

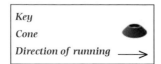

Figure 1.2 Grid variation

DRILL *SPLIT GRID*

Aim
To improve ball control and passing skills.

Area/equipment
Mark out an indoor or outdoor grid 20 yards in length with an additional 10 yards on the end (use different coloured cones). The width of the grid is variable depending on the size of the squad. Place a ball for each player who will have just completed her Dynamic Flex drill.

Description
Perform Dynamic Flex down the grid over the first 20 yards, on reaching the additional 10-yard area perform ball skills up and back over it. On completing the ball skills, pass the ball to the player coming on, who will have just completed her Dynamic Flex drill.

Key teaching points
- The timing is critical – players should be constantly on the move
- Players should communicate with one another, e.g. when passing the ball

Sets and reps
Players can perform the entire Dynamic Flex warm-up in this manner.

Variations/progressions
Vary the ball skill drills.

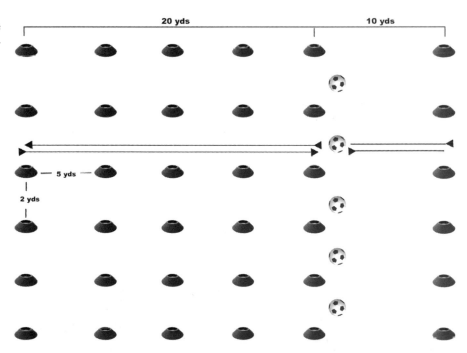

Figure 1.3 Split grid

GRID VARIATIONS

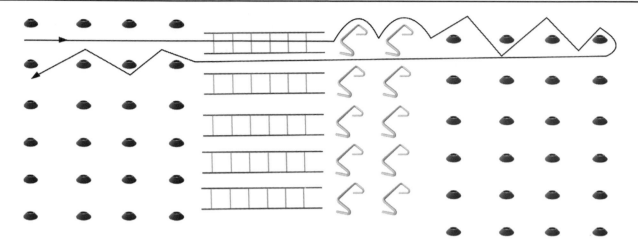

Figure 1.4 Combination warm-up grid 1

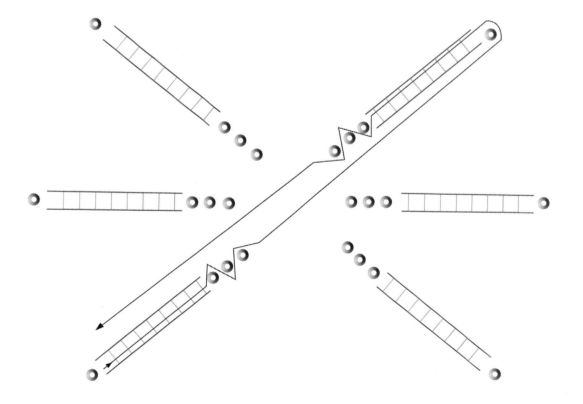

Figure 1.5 Combination warm-up grid 2 – multi-crossover

GRID VARIATIONS

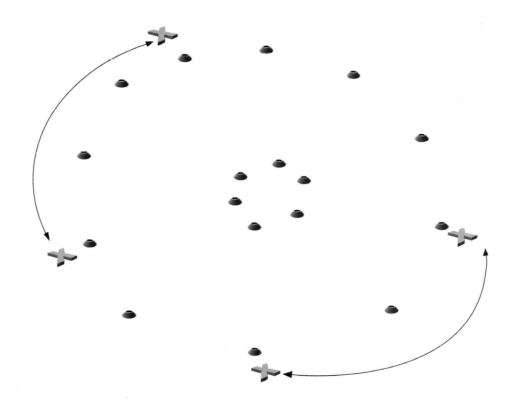

Figure 1.6 Dynamic Flex circle grid

THE MECHANICS OF MOVEMENT

One of the most damaging assumptions made by coaches and managers is that their players have been taught to run correctly or that it is something that occurs naturally. You will always encounter natural, genetically gifted players who are explosive and who make fast running look easy – although these are few and far between. To neglect running mechanics in your soccer training is to ignore the potential in many of your players.

How often one hears comments about players such as: 'good player but too slow', 'she falls back on their heels' or 'not quick enough over the first few yards'. All players, whatever their age, can improve their speed and acceleration by practising and applying the correct running mechanics.

The best players and teams in the world are able to vary the pace of their play effectively. They inject explosive phases and controlled deceleration allowing them to constantly vary the speed of the game to suit the situation. Indeed the physical demands of the women's game are continually changing.

Recent research provides the following statistics on time spent performing various movements in a game of soccer. The figures represent a combination of players playing at different league levels.

stationary	14%
walking	50%
jogging	28%
striding/sprinting	3%

As we might expect the results also highlight the fact that the game is played at a higher tempo in the higher leagues.

The physical demands placed on the female soccer player are complex. Soccer is a multi-sprint activity, therefore players do not run continuously at the same pace. In the course of the game players perform more than 1,000 changes in activity and use over 420 different patterns of movement. The ball is in play for less than 60 minutes in the whole match with average bursts of activity lasting between 3 and 6 seconds and with average distances covered less than 25 yards. An average sprint during a match lasts less than 3 seconds but may be crucial in deciding the outcome of a match. On average a player will touch the ball for less than 2 minutes in a match. The position played on the field also has a bearing on the type, intensity and frequency of running and movements that different players will perform. A forward will sprint more than a mid-fielder, who will cover a greater distance.

Female soccer players will on average cover distances ranging between 5 and 9 miles (8–14.5 km) with intermittent bouts of movement including running, turning, acceleration, deceleration, jumping, running backwards, walking and standing still. All these statistics highlight the importance of the use of correct mechanics in running and all other movement patterns because they affect the player's economy, efficiency and effectiveness of movement when playing soccer.

Arm mechanics

There is no need to focus on techniques for the 100 m sprint. Soccer players very rarely have the space to plain out after 30 m or relax and think about 'jelly jaw' exercises. Soccer requires a sound basic technique, the ability to change from correct running mechanics, to holding off a player, to using the arms for balance with the ball at the feet, back to reasserting good mechanics to re-accelerate.

Remember many coaches and managers are first and foremost looking for the players who are explosive over the first 5 yards. Using the correct arm drive will go a long way to assisting players of all shapes and sizes to be quicker in this area.

Running form

ARMS

- Elbows should be held at 90°

- Hands and shoulders should be relaxed

- The insides of the wrists should brush against the pockets

- The hands should move from the buttock cheeks to the chest or head.

Lift mechanics

Coaching players to get their knees up high particularly in the first few yards of the acceleration phase only makes them slower. Using high knee-lift during the acceleration phase has the negative effect of minimizing force development, therefore not enough power is produced to propel the body forward in an explosive action. During the first few yards of acceleration short, sharp steps are required. These steps generate a high degree of force which takes the body from a stationary position into the first controlled explosive steps.

Soccer is a multi-sprint stop-and-start sport, so the first phase of acceleration and re-acceleration are crucial. Look and listen for the following in a player's initial acceleration strides:

- 45° knee-lift

- Foot-to-floor contact with the ball of the foot

- Front of the foot stays in a linear position

- Knees coming up in a vertical line

- Foot-to-floor contact making a tapping noise, not a thud or slap

- The foot and knee should not splay in or out, or power will not be transferred correctly

- Keep off the heels

- On the lift, the foot will transfer from pointing slightly down to pointing slightly up

Posture

Posture is a crucial part of all movements required for soccer including sprinting, jumping and turning. The spine should be kept as straight as possible at all times. This means that a player who has tackled, jockeyed or jumped for the ball and now has to run into space, needs to transfer to the correct running form as quickly as possible. Running with a straight spine does not mean running bolt upright, you can keep your spine straight using a slight lean forward. What *is* to be avoided is players running while sinking into their hips which looks like being folded up in the middle, or sinking too deep when landing after jumping because this prevents instant effective transfer of power.

Core control is another important factor in developing and utilising a strong posture. Core development and maintenance for women soccer players is very important and will be touched on briefly later in this book. A simple rule prior to and throughout the performing of all the drills in this book is as follows: Engage your core muscles by simply breathing in, breathing out and then breathing in again, try to maintain this feeling throughout the exercise not forgetting to breathe normally! This will help prevent your pelvic wall from moving around which causes a loss of power and will also protect the lower back, hamstrings and girdle area from injury.

Mechanics for deceleration

The ability of a soccer player to stop quickly, change direction and accelerate away from an opponent is a key to building successful teams. You can practise this; do not leave it to chance, include it in your sessions.

- *Posture* – lean back. This alters the angle of the spine and hips which control foot placement. Foot contact with the ground will now transfer to the heel, which acts like a brake

- *Fire the arms* – by firing the arms quickly, the energy produced will increase the frequency of heel contact to the ground. Think of it like pressing harder on the brakes in a car.

The running techniques described in this chapter cover basic mechanics for soccer-specific techniques where running, pushing, jumping and turning are all important parts of the game and are developed through the use of hurdles, stride frequency canes and running technique drills.

Mechanics for Change of Direction Including Lateral and Turning Movements

LATERAL SIDESTEP

Do not use a wide stance as this will decrease the potential for power generation as you attempt to push off/away. Do not pull with the leading foot but rather push off the back foot. Imagine that your car has broken down and that you need to move it to a service station – would you pull it? No you would push it. Ensure that a strong arm drive is used at all times but particularly during the push-off phase.

MAKING A 180° TURN – THE DROP STEP

Most players use too many movements to make a 180° turn. Many jump up on the spot first then take 3 or 4 steps to make the turn, others will jump up and perform the turn in the air with a complete lack of control. When practised, the drop step turn looks seamless and is far quicker.

For a right shoulder turn the player starts by opening up the right groin and simultaneously transferring the weight onto the left foot. The right foot is raised slightly off the ground and, using a swinging action, is moved around to the right to face the opposite direction. The right foot is planted and the player drives/pushes off the left foot remembering to use a strong arm drive. Do not overstretch on the turn. Players may find it helpful initially to tell themselves to 'turn and go'. With practice players will develop an efficient and economic seamless turn.

DRILL | *ARM MECHANICS – PARTNER DRILLS*

Aim
To perfect the correct arm technique for running in soccer.

Area/equipment
The player works with a partner.

Description
The player stands with their partner behind her. The partner holds the palms of her hands in line with the player's elbows, fingers pointing upwards. The player fires the arms as if sprinting so that the elbows smack into their partner's palms.

Key teaching points
- Arms should not move across the body
- Elbows should be at 90°
- Hands and shoulders should be relaxed
- The insides of the wrists should brush against the pockets
- ROM – the hands should move from buttock cheeks to chest or head
- Encourage speed of movement to hear the smack

Sets and reps
3 sets of 16 reps, with 1 minute recovery between each set.

Variations/progressions
Use light hand weights for the first 2 sets, perform the last set without.

DRILL ARM MECHANICS – MIRROR DRILLS

Aim
To perfect the correct arm technique for running in soccer.

Area/equipment
A large mirror.

Description
The player stands in front of the mirror with her arms ready for sprinting and performs short bursts of arm drives. Use the mirror as a feedback tool to perfect the technique.

Key teaching points
- Arms should not move across the body
- Elbows should be at 90°
- Hands and shoulders should be relaxed
- The insides of the wrists should brush against the pockets
- Ensure that the player performs a full ROM – the hands should move from buttock cheeks to chest or head

Sets and reps
3 sets of 16 reps with 1 minute recovery between each set.

Variations/progressions
Use light hand weights for the first 2 sets; perform the last set without.

DRILL ARM MECHANICS – BUTTOCK BOUNCES

Aim
To develop explosive arm drive.

Area/equipment
Suitable ground surface.

Description
The player sits on the floor with her legs straight out in front of her and fires her arms rapidly in short bursts. The power generated should be great enough to raise the buttocks off the floor in a bouncing manner.

Key teaching points
■ Arms should not move across the body
■ Elbows should be at 90°
■ Hands and shoulders should be relaxed
■ The insides of the wrists should brush against the pockets
■ ROM – the hands should move from buttock cheeks to chest or head
■ Encourage speed of movement to hear the smack

Sets and reps
3 sets of 6 reps; each rep is 6–8 explosive arm drives with 1 minute recovery between each set.

Variations/progressions
Use light hand weights for the first 2 sets, perform the last set without.

DRILL RUNNING FORM – DEAD-LEG RUN

Aim
To develop a quick knee-lift and the positive foot placement required for effective sprinting.

Area/equipment
Indoor or outdoor area. Using hurdles, cones or sticks, place approximately 8 obstacles in a straight line at 2-foot intervals. Place a cone 1 yard from each end of the line to mark a start and finish.

Description
The player must keep the outside leg straight in a locked position. The inside leg moves over the obstacles in a cycling motion while the outside leg swings along just above the ground (*see* fig. 2.1).

Key teaching points
- Bring the knee of the inside leg up to just below 90°
- Point the toe upwards
- Bring the inside leg back down quickly between the hurdles
- Increase the speed when the technique has been mastered
- Maintain correct arm mechanics
- Maintain an upright posture and a strong core
- Keep the hips square and stand tall

Sets and reps
1 set of 6 reps, 3 leading with the left leg and 3 with the right.

Variations/progressions
- Use light hand weights – accelerate off the end of the last obstacle and drop the hand weights during this acceleration phase
- Place several different coloured markers 2 yards from the last hurdle at different angles. As the player leaves the last hurdle the coach nominates a marker for the player to accelerate to

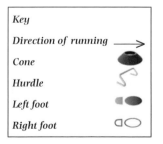

Key

Direction of running ——→

Cone

Hurdle

Left foot

Right foot

Figure 2.1 Dead leg run

DRILL RUNNING FORM – PRE-TURN

Aim
To educate and prepare the hips, legs and feet for effective and quick turning without fully committing the whole body.

Area/equipment
Indoor or outdoor area. Using hurdles, cones or sticks, place about 8 obstacles in a straight line at 2-foot intervals. Place a cone 1 yard from each end of the line to mark a start and finish.

Description
The player moves sideways along the line of obstacles, just in front of them, i.e. not travelling over them (*see* fig. 2.2). The back leg (following leg) is brought over the hurdle to a position slightly in front of the body so that the heel is in line with the toe of the leading foot. As the back foot is planted, the leading foot moves away. Repeat the drill leading with the opposite leg.

Key teaching points
- Stand tall and do not sink into the hips
- Do not allow the feet to cross over
- Keep the feet shoulder-width apart as much as possible
- The knee-lift should be no greater than 45°
- Maintain correct arm mechanics
- Maintain an upright posture
- Keep the hips and shoulders square
- Work both the left and right sides

Sets and reps
1 set of 6 reps, 3 leading with the left shoulder and 3 leading with the right.

Variations/progressions
- Use light hand weights – at the end of the obstacles, turn and accelerate 5 yards. Drop the weights halfway through the acceleration phase
- Place several different coloured markers 2 yards from the last hurdle at different angles. As the player leaves the last hurdle the coach nominates a marker for the player to accelerate to
- Work two players opposite one another and place a ball approximately 5 yards from the last hurdle. As the players leave the last hurdle each races to get to the ball before the other

Key	
Direction of running	→
Cone	
Hurdle	
Left foot	
Right foot	

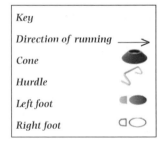

Figure 2.2 Pre-turn

DRILL   RUNNING FORM – LEADING LEG RUN

Aim
To develop quick, efficient steps and running technique.

Area/equipment
Indoor or outdoor area. Using hurdles, cones or sticks, place approximately 8 obstacles in a straight line at 2-foot intervals. Place a cone 1 yard from each end of the line to mark a start and finish.

Description
The player runs down the line of obstacles, crossing over each one with the same lead leg (*see* fig. 2.3). The aim is to just clear the obstacles. Repeat the drill using the opposite leg as the lead.

Key teaching points
- The knee-lift should be no more than 45°
- Use short, sharp steps
- Maintain strong arm mechanics
- Maintain an upright posture
- Stand tall and do not sink into the hips

Sets and reps
1 set of 6 reps, 3 leading with the left leg and 3 leading with the right.

Variations/progressions
- A good exercise for changing direction after running in a straight line is to place 3 cones at the end of the obstacles at different angles 2–3 yards away; on leaving the last obstacle, the player sprints out to the cone nominated by the coach
- Vary the distance between the hurdles to achieve different stride lengths

Key	
Direction of running	→
Cone	
Hurdle	
Left foot	
Right foot	

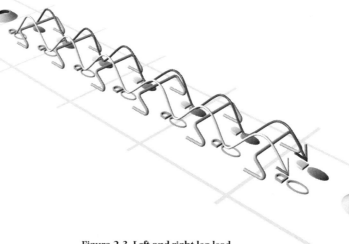

Figure 2.3 Left and right leg lead

DRILL **RUNNING FORM –**
QUICK SIDESTEP DEVELOPMENT

Aim
To develop correct, precise and controlled lateral stepping movements.

Area/equipment
Indoor or outdoor area. Place 3 hurdles side by side about 18 inches apart (*see* fig. 2.4).

Description
The player stands on the outside of either hurdle 1 or hurdle 3 so that she will step over the middle of each hurdle (*see* fig. 2.4). The player performs lateral movements mechanics while clearing each hurdle – on clearing hurdle 3 she repeats the drill in the opposite direction.

Key teaching points
- Maintain correct lateral running form/mechanics
- Maintain correct arm mechanics
- Do not sink into the hips
- Keep the head up
- Do not lean too far forwards
- Use small steps and work off the balls of the feet
- Do not use an excessively high knee-lift

Sets and reps
2 sets of 10 reps, 5 to the left and 5 to the right with a 60 second recovery between sets.

Variations/progressions
- Work with a coach, who should random direct the player over the cones
- Add 2 Macro V Hurdles to add lift variation
- Introduce the ball

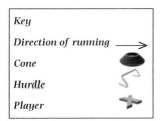

Key

Direction of running ⟶

Cone

Hurdle

Player

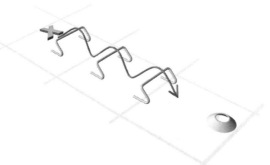

Figure 2.4 Quick sidestep

DRILL — RUNNING FORM – SIDESTEP DEVELOPMENT

Aim
To develop efficient and economical lateral sidesteps.

Area/equipment
Indoor or outdoor area. Place 8 Micro V Hurdles side on, 1 yard apart and staggered laterally (*see* fig. 2.5). Position a finish cone in the same pattern as the hurdles.

Description
The player working inside the channel created by the hurdles steps over each hurdle with one foot as she moves laterally down and across the channel (*see* fig. 2.5). On reaching the end of the channel, walk back to the start and repeat the drill.

Key teaching points
- Bring the knee up to 45° over the hurdle
- Do not 'overstride' across the hurdle
- Maintain correct arm mechanics/strong arm drive
- Keep the hips square
- Do not sink into the hips

Sets and reps
2 sets of 3 reps with a walk-back recovery between reps and 2 minutes between sets.

Variations/progressions
- Perform the drill backwards
- Receive and play the ball in the middle channel before continuing

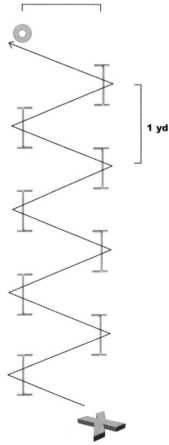

1 yd

1 yd

Figure 2.5 Sidestep

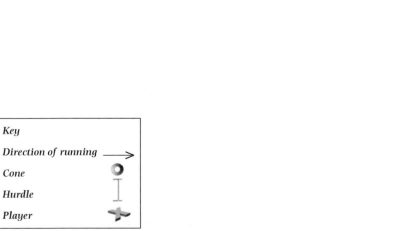

Key

Direction of running →

Cone

Hurdle

Player

DRILL *RUNNING FORM – LATERAL STEP*

Aim
To develop efficient and economical lateral steps.

Area/equipment
Indoor or outdoor area. Using hurdles, cones or sticks, place approximately 8 obstacles in a straight line at 2-foot intervals. Place a cone 1 yard from each end of the line to mark a start and finish.

Description
The player steps over each obstacle while moving sideways (*see* fig. 2.6).

Key teaching points
- Bring the knee up to just below 45°
- Do not skip sideways – step!
- Push off from the back foot
- Do not pull with the lead foot
- Maintain correct arm mechanics
- Maintain an upright posture
- Keep the hips square
- Do not sink into the hips

Sets and reps
1 set of 6 reps, 3 leading with the left shoulder and 3 with the right.

Variations/progressions
- Use light hand weights – accelerate off the end of the last obstacle and drop the hand weights during this phase
- Place several different-coloured markers 2 yards from the last hurdle at different angles. As the player leaves the last hurdle the coach nominates a marker for the player to accelerate to

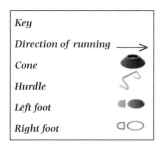

Key	
Direction of running	⟶
Cone	
Hurdle	
Left foot	
Right foot	

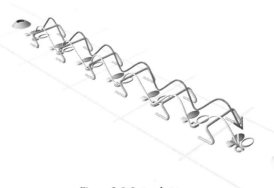

Figure 2.6 Lateral step

DRILL RUNNING FORM – 1-2-3 LIFT

Aim
To develop an efficient leg cycle, rhythm, power and foot placement.

Area/equipment
Indoor or outdoor area 30–40 yards long.

Description
The player moves in a straight line and after every third step the leg is brought up in an explosive action to 90° (*see* fig. 2.7). Continue the drill over the length prescribed working the same leg and then repeat the drill leading with the other leg.

Key teaching points
■ Keep the hips square
■ Work off the balls of the feet
■ Try to develop and maintain a rhythm
■ Keep eyes and head up and look ahead
■ Maintain correct arm mechanics
■ Maintain an upright posture

Sets and reps
1 set of 6 reps, 3 leading with the left leg and 3 with the right.

Variations/progressions
■ Alternate the lead leg during a repetition
■ Vary the lift sequence, e.g. 1-2-3-4-lift, etc.

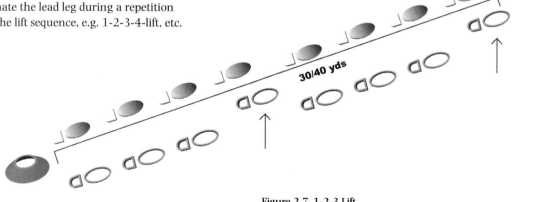

Figure 2.7 1-2-3 Lift

Key
Cone
Left foot
Right foot

DRILL *JUMPING – SINGLE JUMPS*

Aim
To develop jumping techniques, power, speed and control.

Area/equipment
Indoor or outdoor area. Ensure the surface is clear of any obstacles. Use 7- or 12-inch hurdles.

Description
The player jumps over a single hurdle (*see* fig. 2.8(a)) and on landing walks back to the start point to repeat the drill.

Key teaching points
- Maintain good arm mechanics
- Do not sink into the hips at the take-off and landing phases
- Land on the balls of the feet
- Do not fall back onto the heels

Sets and reps
2 sets of 8 reps with 1 minute recovery between each set.

Variations/progressions
- Single jumps over the hurdle and back
- Single jump over the hurdle with a 180° twist (NB: practise twisting to both sides – *see* fig. 2.8(b))
- Lateral single jumps – use both sides to jump off (see fig. 2.8(c))

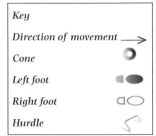

Key	
Direction of movement	⟶
Cone	●
Left foot	◖●
Right foot	◖○
Hurdle	∿

Figure 2.8(a) Two-footed single jump

Figure 2.8(b) Two-footed single jump with 180° twist

Figure 2.8(c) Two-footed lateral single jump

DRILL *JUMPING – MULTIPLE JUMPS*

Aim
To develop maximum control while taking off and landing. To develop controlled directional power.

Area/equipment
Indoor or outdoor area. Place 6–8 hurdles of either 7 or 12 inches in height at 2-foot intervals in a straight line.

Description
The player jumps over each hurdle in quick succession until all hurdles have been cleared (*see* fig. 2.9(a)), then walks back to the start and repeats the drill.

Key teaching points
- Use quick rhythmic arm mechanics
- Do not sink into the hips at the take-off and landing phases
- Land and take off from the balls of the feet
- Stand tall and look straight ahead
- Maintain control
- Gradually build up the speed

Sets and reps
2 sets of 6 reps with 1 minute recovery between each set.

Variations/progressions
- Lateral jumps (*see* fig. 2.9(b))
- Jumps with a 180° twist (*see* fig. 2.9(c))
- Hop over the hurdles, balance, and then repeat (*see* fig. 2.9(d))
- Use light hand weights – for the last rep of each of these sets, perform the drill without the weights as a contrast
- Two forward jumps and one back (*see* fig. 2.9(e))

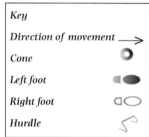

Key	
Direction of movement	→
Cone	◓
Left foot	◖●
Right foot	◖○
Hurdle	⌇

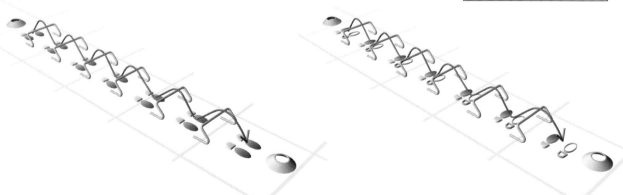

Figure 2.9(a) Multiple jumps   Figure 2.9(b) Lateral jumps

MULTIPLE JUMPS contd.

Figure 2.9(c) Jumps with 180° twist

Figure 2.9(d) Multiple hop

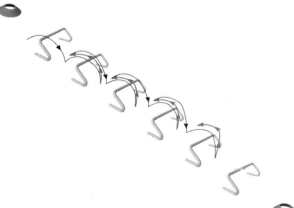

Figure 2.9(e) Two forward jumps and one back

DRILL · *STRIDE FREQUENCY AND STRIDE LENGTH*

Aim

To practice the transfer from the acceleration phase to an increase in stride frequency and length required when running – to develop an efficient leg cycle, rhythm, power and foot placement.

Area/equipment

Indoor or outdoor area, 40–60 yards long. Place 12 coloured 4-foot sticks or canes flat on the ground at 5–6 foot intervals (the intervals will be determined by the size and age of the squad).

Description

Starting 20 yards away from the first stick the player accelerates towards the sticks and aims to land just past each one. After the last stick the player gradually decelerates. Return to the start and repeat the drill.

Key teaching points

- Do not overstride
- Work off the balls of the feet
- Try to develop and maintain a rhythm
- Keep eyes and head up as if looking over a fence
- Maintain correct mechanics
- Maintain an upright posture
- Stay focused
- Alter distances between strides for different ages and heights

Sets and reps

1 set of 4 reps.

Variations/progressions

- Set up the stride frequency sticks as shown in fig. 2.10. The sticks now control the acceleration and deceleration phases
- Add a change of direction during the deceleration phase

Key
Cone
Stick

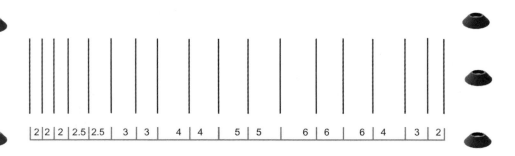

Figure 2.10 Stride frequency/length stick grid

DRILL RUNNING FORM – WITH A BALL

Aim

To maintain good mechanics when faced with soccer-specific stresses with the inclusion of a ball. To improve decision-making ability.

Area/equipment

Indoor or outdoor area. Place 8 hurdles in a straight line at 2 feet intervals. Place a cone at each end approximately 2 yards from the first and last cones respectively.

Description

The coach stands at the end cone with the football. The player performs a mechanics drill through the hurdles and on clearing the final hurdle accelerates on to the ball that has been fed in at various angles by the coach (*see* fig. 2.11(a)).

Key teaching points

■ Maintain correct mechanics
■ Stay focused by looking ahead
■ Fire the arms explosively when accelerating to the ball

Key	
Direction of run	→
Cone	
Hurdle	
Ball	
Coach	
Direction of ball	------>

Sets and reps

3 sets of 6 reps. NB: the sets should be made up various mechanics drills.

Variations/progressions

■ On clearing the final hurdle, the ball is fed to the player at chest height. The player controls the ball and executes a side-foot volley to the coach who lays the ball off for the player to accelerate on to (*see* fig. 2.11(b))
■ The player performs lateral mechanics drills with her back to the coach, the coach also works laterally approximately 2 yards away from the player. The coach feeds the ball to the player who must then turn to the left or right as instructed, gather, control and return the ball (*see* fig. 2.11(c))

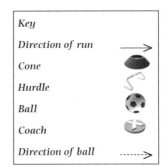

Figure 2.11(a) Running mechanics with ball

RUNNING FORM – WITH A BALL contd.

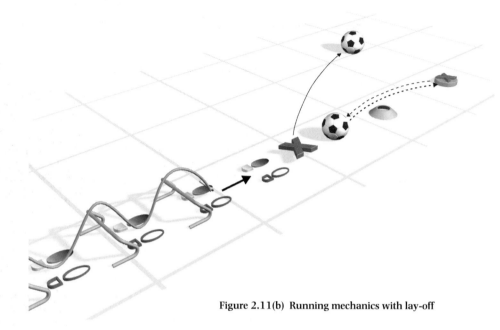

Figure 2.11(b) Running mechanics with lay-off

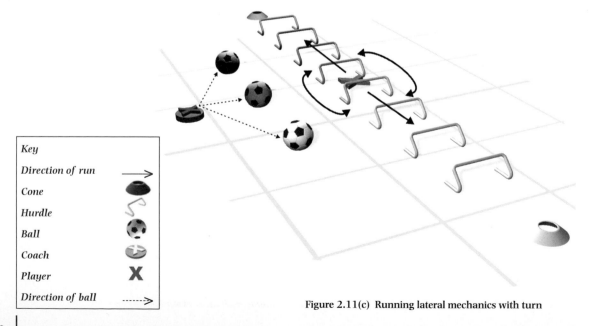

Key	
Direction of run	→
Cone	
Hurdle	
Ball	
Coach	
Player	X
Direction of ball	---->

Figure 2.11(c) Running lateral mechanics with turn

DRILL — RUNNING FORM – HURDLE MIRROR DRILLS

Aim
To improve the performance of mechanics under pressure. To improve random agility.

Area/equipment
Indoor or outdoor area. Mark out a grid with 2 lines of 8 hurdles, with 2 feet between each hurdle and 2 yards between each line of hurdles.

Description
Players face each other while performing mechanics drills up and down the lines of hurdles (*see* fig. 2.12(a)). One player initiates the movements while the partner attempts to mirror those movements. Players can perform both lateral and linear mirror drills.

Key teaching points
▪ Stay focused on your partner
▪ The player mirroring should try to anticipate the lead player's movements
▪ Maintain correct arm mechanics

Sets and reps
Each player performs 3 sets of 30-second work periods. Ensure 30 seconds recovery between each work period.

Variations/progressions
▪ First-to-the-ball drill – as above, except a ball is placed between the 2 lines of hurdles (*see* fig. 2.12(b)). The proactive partner commences the drill as normal then accelerates to the ball, collects it and dribbles to an end cone. The reactive player attempts to beat the proactive player to the ball
▪ Lateral drills performed as above – players work in pairs with only 2 hurdles per player, effective for improving short-stepping, lateral marking skills (*see* figs. 2.12(b) and (c))

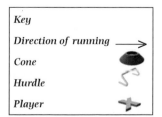

Key	
Direction of running	⟶
Cone	
Hurdle	
Player	

Figure 2.12(a) Hurdle mirror drills

HURDLE MIRROR DRILLS contd.

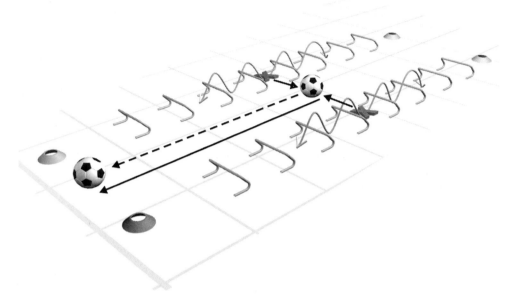

Figure 2.12(b) First-to-the-ball mirror drills

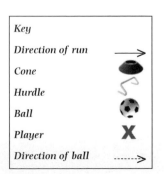

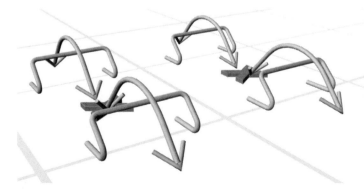

Figure 2.12(c) Short-step mirror drills

DRILL RUNNING FORM – CURVED ANGLE RUN

Aim
To develop controlled, explosive fast feet while running on a curved angle.

Area/equipment
Indoor or outdoor area. Place 10 hurdles in a curved formation, 2 feet apart. Place a cone at each end, approximately 2 yards from the first and last hurdles respectively.

Description
The player performs running drills as already described, the Dead-leg run (*see* page 40), Lateral stepping (*see* page 45) or Leading leg run-throughs – same leg leading over each hurdle.

Key teaching points
■ Work both left and right sides
■ The knee-lift should be no more than 45°
■ Use short, sharp steps
■ Maintain powerful arm mechanics
■ Maintain an upright posture
■ Look ahead at all times

Sets and reps
Each player performs 1 set of 6 reps. Leave 30 seconds recovery between each work rep.

Variations/progressions
■ Introduce the ball
■ Introduce tighter curves
■ Use immediately after straight-run hurdle work

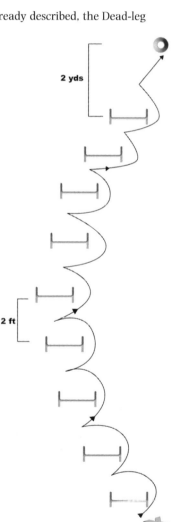

2 yds

2 ft

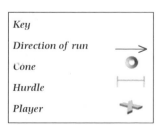

Key

Direction of run →

Cone

Hurdle

Player

Figure 2.13 Curved angle running

DRILL RUNNING FORM – COMPLEX MECHANICS

Aim
To prevent players resorting to bad habits particularly when under pressure. To challenge players by placing them in game-like pressure situations, and to maintain good running form even in the most difficult and demanding of situations.

Area/equipment
Indoor or outdoor area. Place 4 hurdles in a straight line with 2 feet between each hurdle. The next 4 hurdles are set slightly to one side and the final 4 hurdles are placed back in line with the original 4 (*see* fig. 2.14(a)).

Description
The player performs a dead-leg run over the hurdles with the dead leg changing over the 4 centre hurdles. Return to the start by performing the drill over the hurdles in the opposite direction.

Key teaching points
■ Maintain correct arm mechanics
■ Work off the balls of the feet
■ Try to develop and maintain a rhythm
■ Keep eyes and head up and look ahead
■ Maintain correct arm mechanics
■ Maintain an upright posture
■ Keep the hips square

Sets and reps
4 sets of 4 reps.

Variations/progressions
■ Perform the drill laterally moving both forwards and backwards to cross the centre 4 hurdles (see fig. 2.14(b))
■ Place hurdles in a cross formation (see fig. 2.14(c)), and perform drills up to the centre and sideways, left or right, up or across
■ Introduce players from other sides/squads

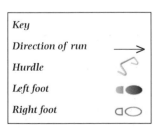

Key	
Direction of run	→
Hurdle	
Left foot	
Right foot	

Figure 2.14(a) Complex mechanics drills

COMPLEX MECHANICS contd.

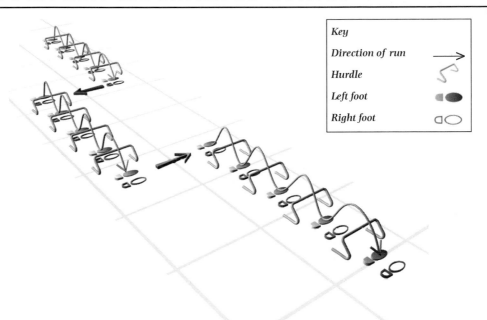

Figure 2.14(b) Complex lateral mechanics drills

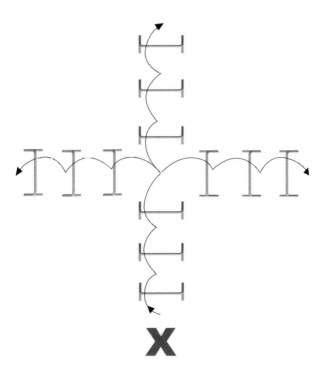

Figure 2.14(c) Cross formation hurdles drill

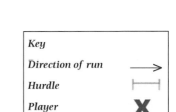

CHAPTER 3　INNERVATION

FAST FEET, AGILITY AND CONTROL FOR SOCCER

Innervation is the transition stage from the warm-up and mechanics to periods of high intensity of work that activate the neural pathways, or, in other words, cause the nerves to fire the muscles as quickly as possible. Using the Fast Foot™ Ladder, dance-like patterns such as twists, jumps and turns are all introduced. Soccer-specific footwork drills that require speed, co-ordination and agility such as sidestep shuffles are practised explosively with and without the football. Also upper body innervation drills for the arms and hands can be implemented here for goalkeepers. The key is to speed up these techniques without compromising the quality of the mechanics.

The innervation drills in this chapter progress from simple footwork patterns to complex soccer-specific drills.

DRILL   *FAST FOOT LADDER – SINGLE RUNS*

Aim
To develop fast feet with control, precision and power.

Area/equipment
Indoor or outdoor area. Use a Fast Foot Ladder – ensure that this is the correct ladder for the type of surface being used.

Description
The player covers the length of the ladder by placing a foot in each ladder space (*see* fig. 3.1(a)). Return to the start by jogging back beside the ladder.

Key teaching points
- Maintain correct running form/mechanics
- Start slowly and gradually increase the speed
- Maintain an upright posture
- Stress that quality not quantity is important

Sets and reps
3 sets of 4 reps with 1 minute recovery between each set.

Variations/progressions
- Single lateral step – as above but performed laterally (*see* fig. 3.1(b))
- In-and-out – moving sideways along the ladder stepping into and out of each ladder space, i.e. both feet in and both feet out (*see* fig. 3.1(c))
- 'Icky shuffle' – sidestepping movement into and out of each ladder space whilst moving forwards (*see* fig. 3.1(d))
- Double run – perform as single run above but with both feet in each ladder space (*see* fig. 3.1(e))
- Hopscotch (*see* fig. 3.1(f))
- Single-space jumps – two-footed jumps into and out of each ladder space (*see* fig. 3.1(g))
- Two forward and one back (*see* fig. 3.1(h))
- 'Spotty Dogs' (*see* fig. 3.1(i))
- 'Twist Again' (*see* fig. 3.1(j))
- Hops in-and-out (*see* fig. 3.1(k))
- Carioca (*see* fig. 3.1(l))

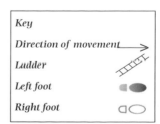

Key	
Direction of movement	→
Ladder	
Left foot	
Right foot	

MULTIPLE JUMPS contd.

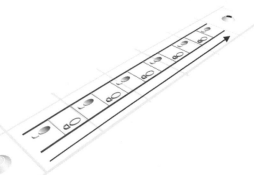

Figure 3.1(a) Single runs

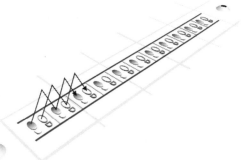

Figure 3.1(b) Single lateral step

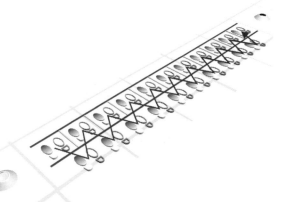

Figure 3.1(c) In-and-out

Figure 3.1(d) 'Icky shuffle'

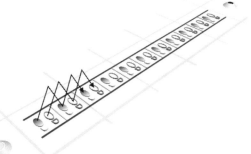

Figure 3.1(e) Double run

Figure 3.1(f) Hopscotch

MULTIPLE JUMPS contd.

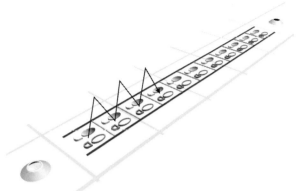

Figure 3.1(g) Single-space jumps

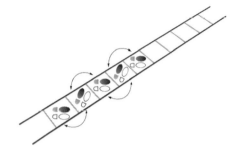

Figure 3.1(j) 'Twist again'

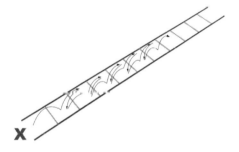

Figure 3.1(h) Two forward and one back

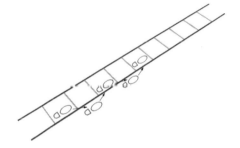

Figure 3.1(k) Hops in-and-out

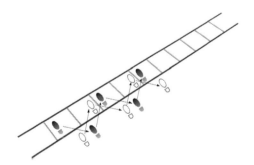

Figure 3.1(i) 'Spotty dogs'

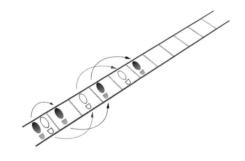

Figure 3.1(l) Carioca

DRILL   *FAST FOOT LADDER – T FORMATION*

Aim
To develop speed of acceleration when pressing the opposition. To develop controlled lateral cross-cover and defensive backward jockeying movements.

Area/equipment
Indoor or outdoor area. Place 2 ladders in a T formation with 3 cones placed at the end of each ladder.

Description
The player accelerates down the ladder using single steps. On reaching the ladder crossing the end, the player moves laterally either left or right using short lateral steps. On coming out of the ladder the player then jockeys backwards towards the start line (*see* fig. 3.2).

Key teaching points
■ Maintain correct running form/mechanics
■ Use strong arm drive when transferring from linear to lateral steps
■ When jockeying backwards keep the head and eyes up

Sets and reps
3 sets of 4 reps with 1 minute recovery between each set (2 moving to the left and 2 to the right)

Variations/progressions
■ Start with a lateral run and upon reaching the end ladder accelerate in a straight line forwards down the ladder
■ Mix and match previous quick feet ladder drills described earlier (*see* page 59)

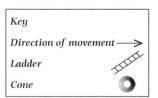

Key
Direction of movement →
Ladder
Cone

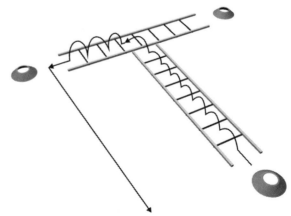

Figure 3.2 Up, across and jockey backwards

DRILL *FAST FOOT LADDER – CROSSOVER*

Aim
To develop speed, agility and change of direction in a more soccer-specific 'crowded' area. To improve reaction time, peripheral vision and timing.

Area/equipment
Large indoor or outdoor area. Place 4 ladders in a cross formation leaving a clear centre square of about 3 square yards. Place a cone 1 yard from the start of each ladder.

Description
Split the squad in to 4 equal groups and locate them at the start of each ladder. Simultaneously players accelerate down the ladder performing a single-step drill, on reaching the end of the ladder players accelerate across the centre square and join the end of the queue. Do not travel down this ladder.

Key teaching points
- Maintain correct running form/mechanics
- Keep the head and eyes up and be aware of other players particularly around the centre area

Sets and reps
3 sets of 6 reps with 1 minute recovery between each set

Variations/progressions
- At the end of the first ladder sidestep to the right or left and join the appropriate adjacent ladder (see fig. 3.3.(b))
- Vary the fast foot ladder drills performed down the first ladder
- Include a 360° turn in the centre square, this is effective for positional awareness

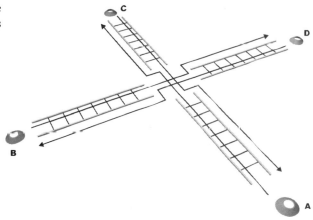

Figure 3.3(a) Crossover drill

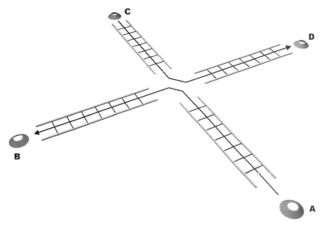

Figure 3.3(b) Crossover drill with sidestep

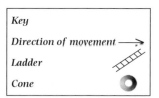

Key

Direction of movement ⟶

Ladder

Cone

DRILL   *FAST FOOT LADDER – MIRROR*

Aim
To develop explosive footwork patterns for blocking and tackling and to improve footwork reactions for close marking situations.

Area/equipment
Indoor or outdoor area. Use 1 15-foot section of ladder.

Description
Player 1 and Player 2 stand opposite each other on either side of the ladder. Starting in the middle, Player 1 moves laterally and randomly steps in and out of the ladder. Player 2 responds by mirroring as quickly and as accurately as possible the movements of Player 1 (*see* fig. 3.4).

Key teaching points
- Maintain correct lateral running form/mechanics
- Use short, sharp explosive steps
- Work off the balls of the feet
- Use a strong arm drive
- Always keep the hips square

Sets and reps
3 sets of 2 reps with a 15-second rest between reps and a 2-minute recovery between each set. NB: In 1 set each player should take the lead for 45 seconds.

Variations/progressions
Introduce slight upper body, game-like contact

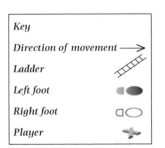

Key	
Direction of movement	→
Ladder	
Left foot	
Right foot	
Player	

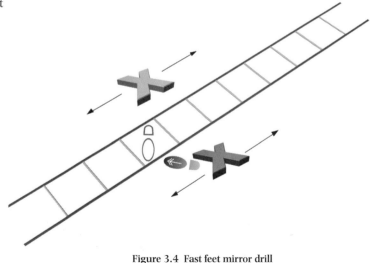

Figure 3.4 Fast feet mirror drill

DRILL | *FAST FOOT LADDER – WITH A BALL*

Aim

To develop fast feet, speed and agility while incorporating game-specific ball control.

Area/equipment

Large indoor or outdoor area. Place a Fast Foot Ladder with a cone about 1 yard away from each end.

Description

While Player 1 is performing fast foot drills down the ladder either laterally or linearly, Player 2, standing 2 yards away from the ladder in a central position, feeds the ball to the player at different heights, requiring Player 1 to perform either a foot, chest or head skill to control and return the ball (*see* fig. 3.5).

Key teaching points

- Concentrate on good footwork patterns
- Ensure that correct technical skills are used when controlling and returning the ball
- Ensure that the player performing the drill reverts to correct running form/mechanics after returning the ball

Sets and reps

3 sets of 6 reps with 1 minute recovery between each set.

Variations/progressions

Vary the fast foot ladder drills performed by the player.

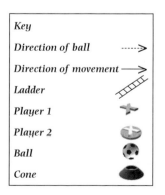

Key	
Direction of ball	---->
Direction of movement	---->
Ladder	
Player 1	
Player 2	
Ball	
Cone	

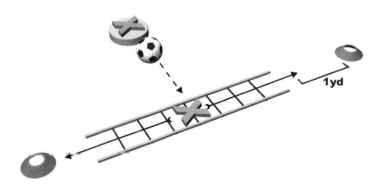

Figure 3.5 Fast Foot Ladder with a ball

65

DRILL FAST FOOT LADDER – WITH PASSING

Aim
To develop fast feet and agility while incorporating soccer-specific ball control and passing combination drills.

Area/equipment
Large indoor or outdoor area. Place 2 sets of ladder sections, each in an upside-down L pattern, next to each other and approximately 2 yards apart. Place a cone 1 yard from the start and end of each ladder. Place another 2 cones 15 yards away and 1 yard apart in line with the centre space. At the end of one ladder, place a ball.

Description
Both players start with linear fast foot drills then transfer to lateral drills as the ladder dictates. Player 1 accelerates onto the ball and dribbles for 2 yards before passing the ball to Player 2 to move on to. On receiving the ball the Player 2 takes just one or two touches before passing the ball back to Player 1, who shoots the ball through the cones (*see* fig. 3.6). Players jog back to the start where they swap roles.

Key teaching points
- Maintain correct running form/mechanics
- Ensure that correct technical skills are used when players are on the ball
- Players should communicate clearly – visual and verbal

Sets and reps
3 sets of 6 reps with 1 minute recovery between each set, i.e. 3 reps as Player 1 and 3 reps as Player 2.

Variations/progressions
Vary the fast foot ladder drills performed linearly and laterally by the players.

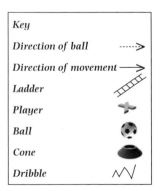

Key	
Direction of ball	---->
Direction of movement	—>
Ladder	
Player	
Ball	
Cone	
Dribble	

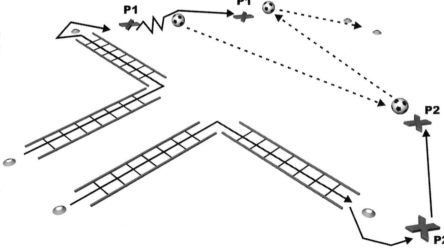

Figure 3.6 Fast Foot Ladder with passing drill

DRILL FAST FOOT LADDER – LATERAL PASSING

Aim
To develop fast foot combination work, acceleration, timing and passing laterally under pressure.

Area/equipment
Large indoor or outdoor area. Place 3 sections of 15-foot ladder and 3 cones as shown in fig. 3.7.

Description
Player 1 accelerates down ladder A, Players 2 and 3 also accelerate down their corresponding ladders B and C. As Player 1 leaves ladder A Coach X will pass a ball for the player to control and pass on to Player 2 who then passes the ball to Player 3 on to Coach Y. On completion of their pass the players accelerate to the cone before decelerating and jogging back to the start. The drill is then repeated from the opposite side.

Key	
Direction of ball	---->
Direction of movement	——>
Ladder	/////
Player	**X**
Ball	●
Cone	◯
Coach	◉

Key teaching points
- Maintain correct running form/mechanics
- Players should communicate
- Good timing of support runs is important
- Good passing techniques are to be used

Sets and reps
3 sets of 5 reps with a slow jog back recovery between reps and a 2-minute recovery between each set.

Variations/progressions
- Vary the ladder drills
- Vary the type of pass

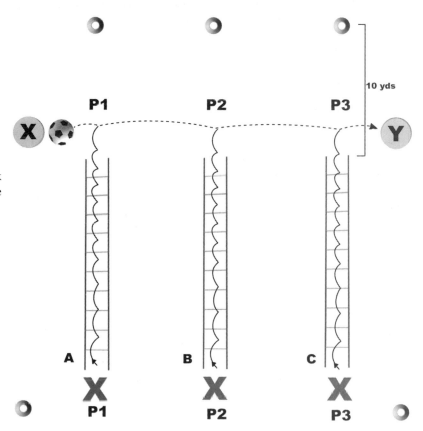

Figure 3.7 Fast Foot Ladder with lateral passing

DRILL FAST FOOT LADDER 'IPSWICH TOWN GRID'

Aim
To develop fast feet, agility and control in a restricted area while under pressure from other players.

Area/equipment
Large indoor or outdoor area. Place 4 ladders side by side.

Description
Working in pairs, players will work down the length of the outside ladders and perform fast foot drills. On the coach's signal the players will move to the centre ladders and work side by side (*see* fig. 3.8(a)).

Key teaching points
- Maintain correct running form/mechanics
- Players should push and nudge each other to simulate the close marking situations that occur in a game
- If players are knocked off balance, they should reassert the correct arm mechanics as soon as possible

Sets and reps
3 sets of 4 reps with 1 minute recovery between each set.

Variations/progressions
- Players start on the centre ladders and work out and back in
- Players start on ladders next to each other on either the left or right of the grid and work across the 4 ladders (*see* fig. 3.8(b))

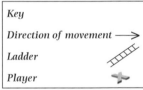

Key	
Direction of movement	⟶
Ladder	
Player	

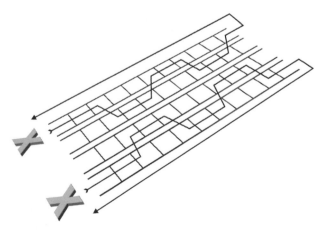

Figure 3.8(a) 'Ipswich Town Grid'

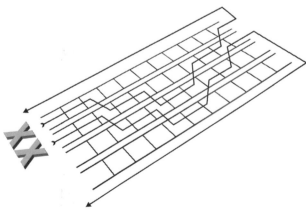

Figure 3.8(b) 'Ipswich Town Grid' progression

DRILL FAST FOOT LADDER GIANT CROSSOVER

Aim
To develop fast feet, speed, agility, co-ordination and visual reaction skills both with and without the ball.

Area/equipment
Large indoor or outdoor area. Place 4 ladders in a cross formation with 25 yards between them in the centre area. Place a ball at the end of one ladder and another at the end of an adjacent ladder.

Description
Split the squad into 4 equal groups and locate them at the start of each ladder. Simultaneously players accelerate down the ladder performing fast foot drills. The 2 players with a ball dribble it across the centre area and pass it to the oncoming player, who receives and controls it before passing to the next oncoming player. Having passed the ball the player joins the queue on the opposite side of the cross without travelling down the opposite ladder (*see* fig. 3.9).

Key teaching points
■ This should be a continuous drill
■ Maintain correct running form/mechanics
■ Correct technical skills must be used when players are on the ball
■ Players should use clear communication

Sets and reps
3 sets of 6 reps with 1 minute recovery between each set.

Variations/progressions
■ Vary the passing drills used in the centre area
■ Vary the amount of control allowed, e.g. one touch, two touches etc.

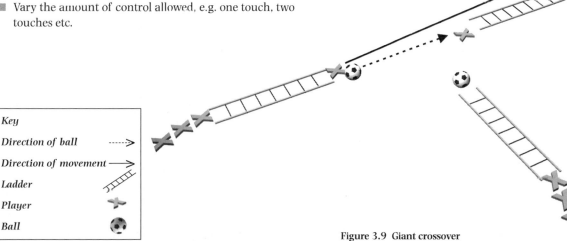

Key
Direction of ball   ----->
Direction of movement   ----->
Ladder
Player
Ball

Figure 3.9 Giant crossover

DRILL FAST FOOT LADDER – LONG PASS

Aim

To develop fast feet, speed, agility and acceleration while focusing on getting into position early to receive a long pass. To develop accurate passing over long distances.

Area/equipment

Large indoor or outdoor area and 4 ladders. Place 2 ladders next to each other 10 yards apart. The other 2 ladders should be placed in the same formation 40–50 yards away. Place a ball at the end of each of the first sets of ladders.

Description

Split the squad into 4 equal groups and locate them at the ends of each ladder so all players are facing the centre space. Players perform nominated fast foot drills down the ladders. Two of the players (at the same end) will collect a ball at the end of their ladder and make a long straight pass to the player coming down the opposite ladder. On completing the pass the player will jockey backwards to the start position (*see* fig. 3.10(a)).

Key teaching points

- Maintain correct running form/mechanics
- Players should use correct technical skills when on the ball
- The timing of the player who is to receive the ball is crucial – she should receive the ball just as she leaves the ladder to enter the centre space
- The player receiving the ball should do so on the move *not* while standing still

Sets and reps

3 sets of 6 reps with 1 minute recovery between each set.

Variations/progressions

- Make the long pass a diagonal one
- For sprint endurance conditioning, the players accelerate across the centre space (*see* fig. 3.10(b))

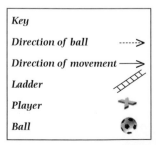

Key	
Direction of ball	---->
Direction of movement	⟶
Ladder	
Player	
Ball	⚽

FAST FOOT LADDER – LONG PASS contd.

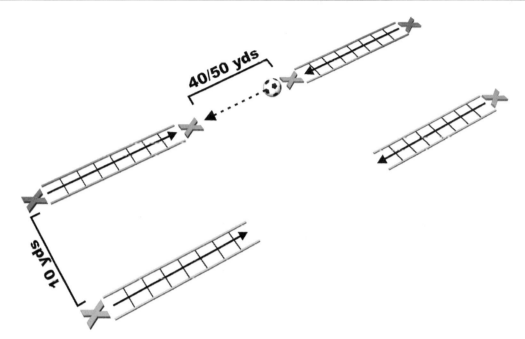

Figure 3.10(a) Fast foot long pass

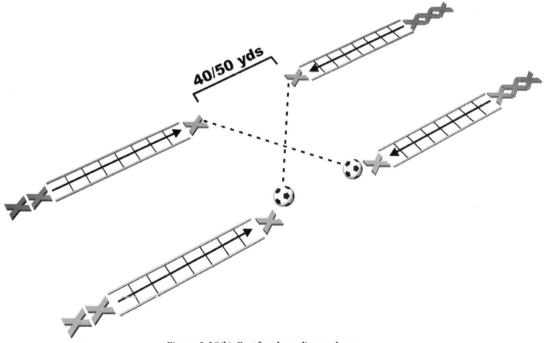

Figure 3.10(b) Fast foot long diagonal pass

DRILL — LINE DRILLS

Aim
To develop quickness of the feet.

Area/equipment
Indoor or outdoor area. Use any line marked on the ground.

Description
The player performs single split steps over the line and back (*see* fig. 3.11(a)).

Figure 3.11(b) Two-footed jumps

Key teaching points
■ Maintain good arm mechanics
■ Maintain an upright posture
■ Maintain a strong core
■ Try to develop a rhythm
■ Keep the head and eyes up

Sets and reps
3 sets of 20 reps with 1 minute recovery between each set.

Figure 3.11(c) Astride jumps

Variations/progressions
■ Two-footed jumps over the line and back (*see* fig. 3.11(b))
■ Stand astride the line and bring the feet in to touch the line before moving them out again. Perform the drill as quickly as possible (*see* fig. 3.11(c))
■ Two-footed side jumps over the line and back (*see* fig. 3.11(d))
■ Two-footed side jumps with a 180° twist in the air over the line and back (*see* fig. 3.11(e))
■ Single quick hops
■ Complex variation – introduce the ball either at the end of the drill for the player to explode on to, or during the drill for her to pass back before continuing

Figure 3.11(d) Two-footed side jumps

Key	
Direction of movement	→
Left foot	◖●
Right foot	◖○

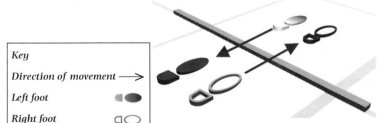

Figure 3.11(a) Single split steps

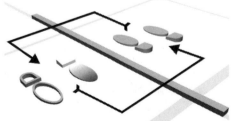

Figure 3.11(e) Two-footed side jumps with twist

DRILL QUICK BOX STEPS

Aim
To develop explosive power and control. NB: The emphasis is on speed.

Area/equipment
Indoor or outdoor area – a bench, aerobics step or suitable strong box with a non-slip surface, about 12 inches high.

Description
The player performs an alternated split step on the box, i.e. one foot on the box and one on the floor (*see* fig. 3.12(a)).

Key teaching points
- Focus on good arm drive
- Maintain an upright posture
- Maintain a strong core
- Keep the head/eyes up
- Work off the balls of the feet
- Work at a high intensity level
- Try to develop a rhythm

Sets and reps
3 sets of 20 reps with 1 minute recovery between each set.

Variations/progressions
- Two-footed jumps on and off the box (*see* fig. 3.12(b))
- Two-footed side jumps on and off the box (10 reps leading with the left shoulder and 10 with the right (*see* fig. 3.12(c))
- Straddle jumps (*see* fig. 3.12(d))
- Single-footed hops onto the box and off (10 reps leading with the left foot and 10 with the right) (*see* fig. 3.12(e))
- Alternate single hop – single hop onto the box to land on the opposite foot. Take off to land on the other side of the box, again on the opposite foot (*see* fig. 3.12(f))

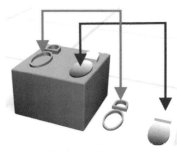

Figure 3.12(c) Two-footed side jumps

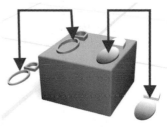

Figure 3.12(d) Straddle jumps

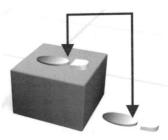

Figure 3.12(e) Single-footed hops

Figure 3.12(f) Alternate single hop

Figure 3.12(a) Split-step jump

Figure 3.12(b) Two-footed jump

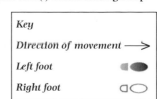

Key	
Direction of movement	⟶
Left foot	
Right foot	

CHAPTER 4 ACCUMULATION OF POTENTIAL

THE SAQ SOCCER CIRCUIT

This is the part of the continuum where we bring together these areas of work already practised. Many of the mechanics and fast-foot drills are specific to developing that skill. In soccer the skills are not isolated but clustered. An example of this is where a player needs to run mechanically well for 30 yards, decelerate, move with fast feet to change direction, jump, turn, sidestep and then stop and assess the situation. These manoeuvres may occur over a varying period of time.

Using ladders, hurdles, cones and poles, etc., soccer-specific circuits can be used to develop programmed agility as well as conditioning the player for this type of high intensity work.

Do not use this phase to fatigue the players. Ensure that a maximum recovery period is implemented between sets and reps.

DRILL   T-RUNS

Aim
To develop soccer-specific speed and agility.

Area/equipment
Indoor or outdoor area. Place 4 poles or cones 5 yards apart in a T formation (*see* fig. 4.1(a)).

Description
The player starts on the left-hand side of the first pole and accelerates to the pole directly ahead. The player should pass this pole and turn to her right before accelerating on to the end pole. She then runs around the end pole and returns to the middle pole before finishing at the opposite side on the start position (*see* fig. 4.1(b)). Repeat the drill by starting on the right of the first pole and turning to the left at the middle pole.

Key teaching points
- Maintain correct running form/mechanics
- Work on shortening the steps used in the turn
- Focus on increasing the speed of the arm drive when coming out of the turns
- Players should work their weak sides – most will have a preferred turning side

Sets and reps
3 sets of 5 reps with 30 seconds recovery between each rep and 1 minute recovery between each set.

Variations/progressions
The coach stands at the centre cone. The player accelerates towards the coach, who provides a verbal or visual signal to dictate which way the player turns.

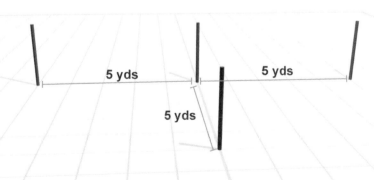

5 yds   5 yds

5 yds

Figure 4.1(a) T-run grid

T-RUNS cont.

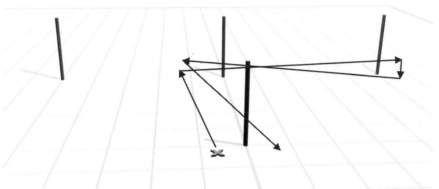

Figure 4.1(b) T-run right

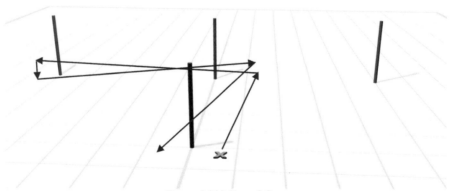

Figure 4.1(c) T-run left

Key

Direction of running ⟶

Player

DRILL *SWERVE-DEVELOPMENT RUNS*

Aim

To develop fine-angle running at pace as if trying to lose a close marker or to create space to receive a ball.

Area/equipment

A large indoor or outdoor area. Place 8–12 poles or cones in a zigzag formation (*see* fig 4.2). The distance between them should be 2–4 yards at varying angles (this will make the runs more realistic). The total length of the run will be 25–30 yards.

Description

The player accelerates from the first cone and swerves in and around all the cones before completing the course. She gently jogs back to the starting cone before repeating the drill.

Key teaching points

- Maintain correct running form/mechanics
- Work on shortening the steps used in the turn
- Focus on increasing the speed of the arm drive when coming out of the turns
- Players should not take wide angles around the cones
- Keep the head and eyes up

Sets and reps

3 sets of 5 reps, with 30 seconds recovery between each rep and 1 minute recovery between each set.

Variations/progressions

Use light hand weights for the first 4 reps then perform the last rep without the weights as a contrast.

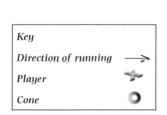

Key	
Direction of running	→
Player	✦
Cone	●

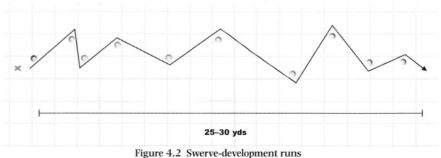

25–30 yds

Figure 4.2 Swerve-development runs

DRILL   AGILITY RUNS – 4-CORNER BALL

Aim

To develop multi-directional explosive agility, turn mechanics and running mechanics both with and without the ball.

Area/equipment

Indoor or outdoor area of about 10 square yards. Place 5 cones, 1 on each corner and 1 in the middle of the square.

Description

The player starts at the centre cone E, then accelerates out to and around cone A and back to cone E. She then completes the drill by going out and around cones B, C and D (this is 1 repetition) (*see* fig. 4.3).

Key teaching points

- Maintain correct running form/mechanics
- Use strong arm mechanics both with and without the ball
- Keep tight to the cones on the turns
- Use short steps on the turns
- Work off the balls of the feet

Sets and reps

3 sets of 2 reps with 1 minute recovery between reps and 2 minutes recovery between sets.

Variations/progressions

- Players run up to the cone and then jockey backwards to cone E
- Players run up to the cone, turn sharply and then sprint back to cone E
- Introduce a ball on cones A, B, C and D so that players pick each ball up in turn and dribble it back to cone E

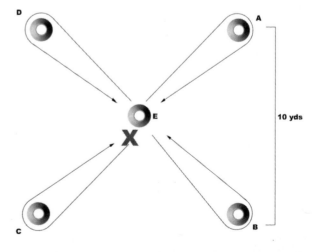

10 yds

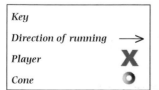

Key

Direction of running ⟶

Player   **X**

Cone   O

Figure 4.3 4-corner ball

DRILL   W-DRILL

Aim
To develop controlled speed, agility and quickness at different angles going both forwards and backwards.

Area/equipment
Indoor or outdoor area. Place 5 cones in a W formation and a further 2 cones as start markers (*see* fig. 4.4(a)).

Description
The player starts at cone 1 and accelerates to cone A. She then completes the W drill by going around each of the cones B, C, D and E using a forwards and backwards movement. Finish the drill at cone E, walk back to cone 2 before repeating the drill in the reverse direction (*see* fig. 4.4(b)).

Key teaching points
- Maintain correct running form/mechanics
- Maintain a strong core
- Use a strong arm drive particularly during acceleration and deceleration phases
- Keep on the balls of the feet particularly when moving backwards
- Use short steps when approaching and working around the cones
- Keep the head and eyes facing forwards – do not look over the shoulder

Sets and reps
3 sets of 6 reps with a walk-back recovery between each rep and 2 minutes recovery between each set.

Variations/progressions
- Players run up to the cones and jockey backwards
- Players complete the drill laterally
- Introduce a ball
- Work in pairs facing each other so that one player works forwards and the other backwards

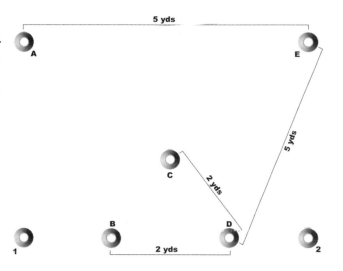

Figure 4.4(a) W-formation

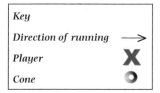

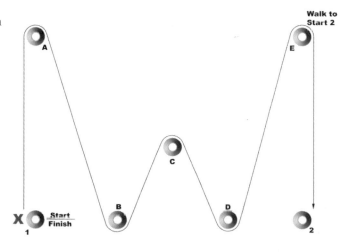

Figure 4.4(b) W-formation drill

DRILL ZIGZAG RUNS

Aim
To develop fast, controlled and angled lateral runs.

Area/equipment
Indoor or outdoor area. Mark out a grid using 10–12 cones or poles in 2 lines of 5–6. Stagger them so that the line is a zigzag formation (*see* fig. 4.5(a)).

Key	
Direction of running	→
Player	**X**
Cone	O
Ladder	

Description
The player runs the zigzag formation, staying on the inside of the cones, and then walks back to the start before repeating the drill.

Key teaching points
- Maintain correct running form/mechanics
- Players must keep their hips facing the direction they are running
- Use short steps
- Do not skip
- Use good arm mechanics

NB: Arm mechanics are as vital in lateral movements as they are in linear movements; many players forget to use their arms when they are moving sideways

Sets and reps
3 sets of 6 reps with a walk-back recovery between each rep and 1 minute recovery between each set.

Variations/progressions
- Perform the drill backwards, performing the jockeying movement
- Players to go around each cone rather that staying on the inside of them
- Up-and-back – enter the grid sideways and move forwards to the first cone then backwards to the next, etc.
- Add a fast foot ladder to the start and finish for acceleration and deceleration running (*see* fig. 4.5(b)).

Figure 4.5(a) Zigzag run

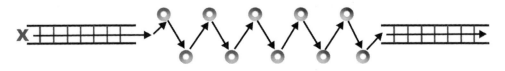

Figure 4.5(b) Ladder zigzag run

DRILL   SOCCER-SPECIFIC RUNS

Aim
To develop soccer-specific running patterns likely to be encountered in games.

Area/equipment
Half a soccer pitch with cones, hurdles, Fast Foot Ladders, poles and footballs. These are all to be placed in a circuit within the area (*see* fig. 4.6).

Key	
Direction of running	→
Player	X
Cone	●
Ladder	
Hurdle	

Description
The players follow a direction that will take them through ladders, stepping and jumping over hurdles, sidestepping through cones, running backwards, jumping, turning and ball skills. NB: One circuit should take players 30–60 seconds to complete.

Key teaching points
Maintain correct running form/mechanics for all activities.

Sets and reps
1 set of 6 reps with a varied recovery time between each rep depending on the stage in the season.

Variations/ progressions
The coach should use her or his imagination to add or subtract obstacles and vary the drills within the circuit in order to keep players motivated and challenged.

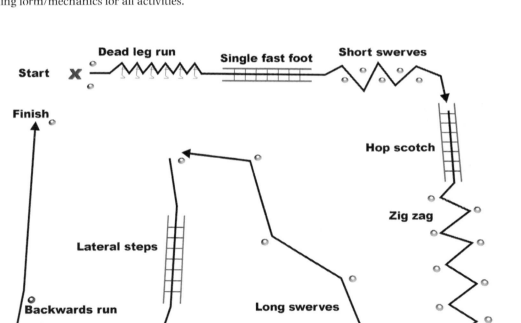

Figure 4.6 Soccer-specific runs

CHAPTER 5 EXPLOSION

3-STEP MULTI-DIRECTIONAL ACCELERATION FOR SOCCER

The exercises detailed in this chapter have been designed to boost response times and develop multi-directional, explosive movements. Programmable and random agility is trained using resisted and assisted high-quality plyometrics. Upper body speed and power is also catered for with jelly ball work outs, effective for developing the type of strength required to hold off an opponent.

The most crucial element of using explosive drills is the implementation of the contrast phase. This simply means performing the drill without resistance for 1 or 2 reps directly after performing them with resistance. These movements will naturally be more explosive and more easily remembered and reproduced.

The key is to ensure that quality, not quantity, is the priority. Efforts must be carefully monitored.

> This is a time for fast action, not tongue-hanging-out fatigue.

DRILL SEATED FORWARD GET-UP

Aim
To develop multi-directional explosive acceleration. To improve a player's ability to get up and accelerate all in one movement.

Area/equipment
Indoor or outdoor area of 20 square yards.

Description
The player sits on the floor, facing the direction she is going to run in with her legs straight out in front of her. On the signal from the coach the player gets up as quickly as possible, accelerates for 10 yards and then slows down before jogging gently back to the start position.

Key teaching points
- Try to complete the drill in one smooth action
- Use correct running form/mechanics
- Do not stop between getting up and starting to run
- Get into an upright position and drive the arms as soon as possible
- Ensure the initial steps are short and powerful
- Do not overstride

Sets and reps
3 sets of 5 reps with a jog-back recovery between each rep and 2 minutes recovery between each set.

Variations/progressions
- Seated backward get-ups
- Seated sideways get-ups
- Lying get-ups from the front, back, left and right
- Kneeling get-ups
- Work in pairs and have get-up competitions chasing the ball
- Work in pairs with one player in front of the other and perform 'tag' get-ups

DRILL LET-GOES

Aim
To develop explosive acceleration and change of direction.

Area/equipment
Indoor or outdoor area – ensure there is plenty of room for safe deceleration. NB: Strong clothing is preferred; if players are wearing light clothing then a towel can be used.

Description
Working in pairs, Player 1 stands directly in front of her partner, Player 2, and grips her shorts or shirt on both sides. Player 1 tries to accelerate away from Player 2 who resists the movement for a few seconds before releasing Player 1. Player 1 accelerates away for 5–8 yards before decelerating and walking back to the start position.

Key teaching points
- Try and get into the correct running posture as soon as possible
- Keep the head up
- Use small initial steps and an explosive arm drive
- Work off the balls of the feet

Sets and reps
3 sets of 6 reps with a jog-back recovery between each rep and 2 minutes active recovery between each set where Player 1 provides the resistance for Player 2.

Variations/progressions
- Lateral let-goes
- Backward lateral let-goes
- Resistance from in front by placing one's hands on one's partner's shoulders and then moving to the side to let her accelerate away

DRILL | *CHAIR GET-UPS*

Aim
To develop explosive power for acceleration linearly and laterally.

Area/equipment
Indoor or outdoor area with plenty of room for deceleration – place a chair/stool and 5 cones as shown in fig. 5.1.

Description
The player sits on the chair and on the coach's signal will get up and move to the nominated cone as quickly as possible. On reaching the cone the player should decelerate and walk back to the start position.

Key teaching points
- Use an explosive arm drive when getting up
- Get into a correct running posture as quickly as possible
- Initial steps should be short and powerful
- Work off the balls of the feet

Sets and reps
3 sets of 10 reps with a walk-back recovery between each rep and 2 minutes recovery between each set.

Variations/progressions
Introduce a 1:2 passing drill at the cones.

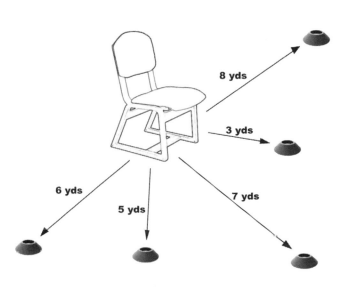

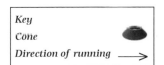

Key
Cone
Direction of running ⟶

Figure 5.1 Chair get-ups

DRILL FLEXI-CORD – BUGGY RUN

Aim
To develop multi-directional explosive acceleration.

Area/equipment
Indoor or outdoor area – ensure that there is plenty of room for safe deceleration. 1 Viper Belt with a Flexi-cord attached at both ends by 2 anchor points. Place 3 cones in a line with 10 yards between each.

Description
Working in pairs, Player 1 wears the belt while Player 2 stands behind holding the Flexi-cord with the hands looped in and over the Flexi-cord (for safety). Player 2 allows the cord to resist as Player 1 accelerates forward then runs behind at a distance sufficient to maintain a constant resistance over the first 10 yards. Both players need to decelerate over the second 10 yards. Player 1 removes the belt after the required number of reps and completes a contrast run on her own. Repeat the drill but swap roles.

Key teaching points
- Player 1 must focus on correct running form/mechanics and explosive drive
- Player 2 works with, not against Player 1, allowing the Flexi-cord to provide the resistance

Sets and reps
1 set of 6 reps plus 1 contrast run with 30 seconds recovery between each rep and 3 minutes recovery before the next exercise.

Variations/progressions
- Lateral buggy run – Player 1 accelerates laterally for the first 2 yards before turning to cover the remaining distance linearly
- After the acceleration phase of the contrast run, the coach can introduce a ball for the player to run on to

DRILL   FLEXI-CORD – OUT AND BACK

Aim
To develop short, explosive, angled accelerated runs – ideal for beating an opponent to the ball or into a space.

Area/equipment
Large indoor or outdoor area of 10 square yards would be ideal. Place 5 cones as shown in fig. 5.2(a), 1 Viper Belt with a Flexi-cord attached to only 1 anchor point on the belt and a safety belt on the other end of the Flexi-cord.

Description
Working in pairs, Player 1 wears the Viper Belt; Player 2 stands directly behind Player 1 holding the Flexi-cord and wearing the safety belt. The Flexi-cord should be taut prior to the drill commencing. Player 2 nominates a cone for Player 1 to run to varying the calls between the 3 cones for the required number of repetitions. When Player 1 arrives at the nominated cone a coach or a third player delivers a ball either to the head, chest or foot to be controlled and passed back before Player 1 returns to the start gate using short, sharp steps. Finish with a contrast run before swapping roles. (*See* fig. 5.2(b).)

Key teaching points
- Focus on short, sharp explosive steps and a fast powerful arm drive
- Maintain correct running form/mechanics
- Work off the balls of the feet
- Use short steps while returning back to the start to help develop balance and control

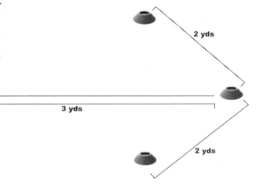

Figure 5.2(a) Flexi-cord out-and-back grid

Sets and reps
3 sets of 6 reps plus 1 contrast run per set with 3 minutes recovery between each set. For advanced players, depending on the time of the season, increase to 9 reps.

Variations/progressions
- Perform the drill laterally
- Jockey backwards with short, sharp steps
- Perform the drill backwards

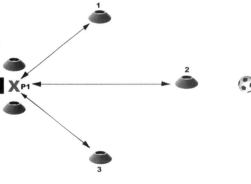

Key	
Cone	
Direction of running	>
Player	X
Coach	
Flexi-cord	::::::::::

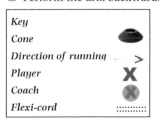

Figure 5.2(b) Flexi-cord out-and-back drill

DRILL FLEXI-CORD – LATERAL BALL WORK

Aim
To develop explosive lateral movements with the ball at the feet.

Area/equipment
Indoor or outdoor area. Place 12 cones in a zigzag formation (*see* fig. 5.3). Position 2 cones to indicate the unscratched Flexi-cord and safety belt distance (approximately 10–12 feet) to act as a guide for the partner.

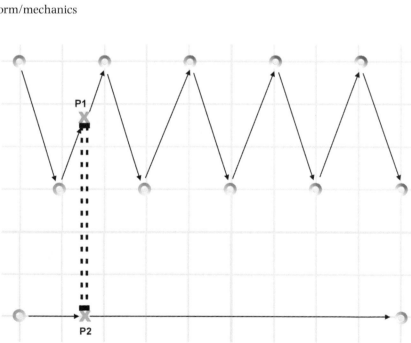

Description
Player 1, wearing the Viper Belt, runs a zigzag pattern between the cones dribbling the ball at her feet. Player 2 works along the line between the 2 outside cones slightly behind the partner to ensure that the Flexi-cord does not get in the way of the arm mechanics. Work up and back along the line of zigzag cones. On completing the reps, Player 1 removes the belt and performs 1 contrast run.

Key teaching points
- Use short, sharp steps. Do not bring the feet too close together or allow them to cross over
- Maintain correct lateral running form/mechanics
- Do not skip
- Push off with the back foot, do not pull with the front foot

Sets and reps
3 sets of 6 reps plus 1 contrast run per set (work both the left and right sides, i.e. just turn the belt around on the player's waist) with 3 minutes recovery between each set.

Variations/progressions
Perform the drill backwards.

Key	
Cone	◎
Direction of running	→
Player	**X**
Flexi-cord	⋯⋯⋯

Figure 5.3 Flexi-cord lateral ball work

DRILL   *FLEXI-CORD – VERTICAL POWER*

Aim
To develop vertical take-off power for the production of more air time and height when jumping to head the ball or to catch the ball as a goalkeeper.

Area/equipment
Indoor or outdoor area approximately 3–4 square yards. 1 Viper Belt with 2 Flexi-cords and a ball.

Description
Work in groups of 4. 1 player wears the Viper Belt which has a Flexi-cord attached by both ends, one end attached to either side of the Viper Belt (*see* photo). Players stand a yard away, one either side of the resisted player; they stand on the Flexi-cord with their legs approximately 1 yard apart. The fourth player stands in front of the resisted player holding the ball above her head. The resisted player jumps to head the ball before regaining position to repeat the drill.

Key teaching points
- Maintain correct jumping form/mechanics
- Do not sink into the hips either before take-off or on landing
- Work off the balls of the feet
- On landing regain balance before the next jump

Sets and reps
3 sets of 8 reps plus 1 contrast jump with 3 minutes recovery between each set.

Variations/progressions
Quick jumps – i.e. no repositioning between jumps. These are fast, repetitive jumps performed as quickly as possible.

DRILL FLEXI-CORD – OVERSPEED

Aim
To develop lightning-quick acceleration.

Area/equipment
Indoor or outdoor area; 4 cones; 1 Viper Belt with a Flexi-cord attached. Place the cones in a T formation with 3 yards between each (*see* fig. 5.4).

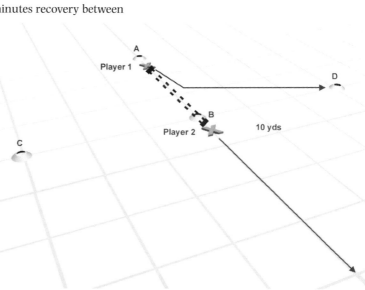

Description
Working in pairs, Player 1 wears the Viper Belt and faces her partner (2) who holds the Flexi-cord and has the safety belt around her waist – i.e. the Flexi-cord will go from belly button to belly button. Player 1 stands at cone A. Player 2 stands at cone B and walks backwards and away from Player 1 thus increasing the Flexi-cord resistance. After stretching the Flexi-cord for 4–5 yards, Player 1 accelerates towards Player 2 who then nominates either cone C or D, requiring Player 1 explosively to change direction. Both players walk back to the start and repeat the drill.

Key teaching points
- Maintain correct running form/mechanics
- Control the running form/mechanics
- During the change of direction phase, shorten the steps and increase the rate of firing in the arms

Sets and reps
3 sets of 8 reps plus 1 contrast run with 3 minutes recovery between each set.

Variations/progressions
- Player 1 starts with a horizontal jump before accelerating away
- Introduce the ball for the player to run on to after the change of direction phase

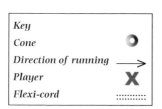

Key
Cone
Direction of running
Player
Flexi-cord

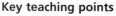

Figure 5.4 Flexi-cord overspeed

DRILL *SIDE-STEPPER – EXPLOSIVE DRILLS*

Aim
To develop multi-directional explosive power.

Area/equipment
Indoor or outdoor 20-yard grid and a Side-Stepper.

Description
The player wearing the Side-Stepper covers the length of the grid by performing high-knee skips. On completing a run she turns around and works back along the grid. The player completes 4 lengths of the grid before removing the Side-Steppers and performing a contrast run.

Key teaching points
- Work off the balls of the feet
- Use a strong arm and knee drive
- Try to develop a rhythmic skip
- Keep the head up and maintain a good posture

Sets and reps
3 sets of 4 reps/lengths of the grid plus 1 contrast run with 3 minutes recovery between each set.

Variations/progressions
- Ice skating
- Lateral wide steps
- Carioca
- Sprinting

DRILL   SIDE-STEPPER – RESISTED LATERAL RUNS

Aim
To develop explosive, controlled lateral patterns of running.

Area/equipment
Indoor or outdoor area. Place 10–12 cones in a zigzag pattern (*see* fig. 5.5) and a Side-Stepper.

Description
The player wearing the SideStepper covers the length of the grid by running a lateral zigzag pattern between the cones. Just before arriving at the cone, extend the last step to increase the level of resistance. On completing a run, turn around and work back along the grid.

Key teaching points
- Maintain correct lateral running form/mechanics
- Do not sink into the hips when stepping off to change direction
- During the directional change phase, increase arm speed to provide additional control

Sets and reps
3 sets of 6 reps plus 1 contrast run with 3 minutes recovery between each set.

Variations/progressions
- Perform the drill backwards – i.e. jockeying movement
- Include the ball

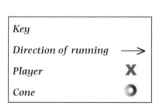

Key	
Direction of running	→
Player	X
Cone	O

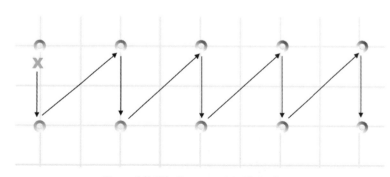

Figure 5.5 Side-Stepper resisted lateral runs

DRILL   SIDE-STEPPER – JOCKEYING IN PAIRS

Aim
To develop woman-to-woman marking skills with particular focus on defensive and attacking jockeying skills.

Area/equipment
Indoor or outdoor area, 6–8 cones. Mark out a channel approximately 20 yards long and 3 yards wide.

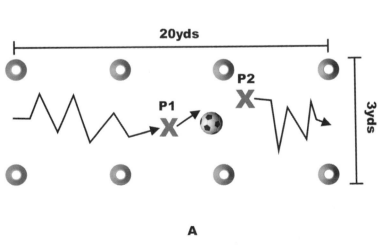

Description
Two players wearing Side-Steppers face each other with about 2 yards between them. The attacking player (1) moves from right to left in a jockeying pattern while the defending player (2) attempts to mirror the movements, preventing the attacking player from having too much space. That is, the attacking player works in a forwards direction and the defending player works backwards.

Key teaching points
- Use quick, low steps *not* high knees
- Do not skip or jump – one foot should be in contact with the floor at all times
- Try to keep the feet shoulder-width apart
- Use a powerful arm drive
- Do not sink into the hips

Sets and reps
3 sets of 4 reps with 30 seconds recovery between each rep and 2 minutes recovery between each set.

Variations/progressions
- Both players perform the drill laterally with one player leading and the other trying to mirror the movements
- Introduce a ball for drill progression (*see* fig. 5.6)

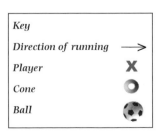

Key	
Direction of running	$\longrightarrow$
Player	**X**
Cone	⊙
Ball	⚽

20yds

P2

P1

3yds

A

Figure 5.6 Side-Stepper resisted jockeying drills

DRILL HAND-WEIGHT DROPS

Aim

To develop explosive power, re-acceleration and, specifically, a powerful arm drive.

Area/equipment

Indoor or outdoor area; 3 cones; hand weights (2–4 lb). Position 1 cone to mark the start, a second 15 yards away and a final cone 10 yards away from the second.

Description

The player with the weights in her hands accelerates to the second cone where she releases the hand weights, keeping a natural flow to the arm mechanics. Continue to accelerate to the third cone before decelerating and walking back to the start before repeating the drill.

Key teaching points

- Maintain correct running form/mechanics
- Do not stop the arm drive to release the weights
- Keep the head tall
- Quality not quantity is vital

Sets and reps

3 sets of 4 reps with 3 minutes recovery between each set.

Variations/progressions

- On the release of the hand weights the coach can call a change of direction – i.e. the player is to accelerate off at different angles
- Perform the drill backwards over the first 15 yards then turn, accelerate and release the weights to explode away
- Perform the drill laterally over the first 15 yards then turn, accelerate and release the weights to explode away

DRILL PARACHUTE RUNNING

Aim
To develop explosive running over longer distances (sprint endurance) and explosive acceleration.

Area/equipment
Indoor or outdoor area, 4 cones and a parachute. Mark out a grid of 50 yards in length, place one cone down as a start marker, and 3 further cones at distances of 30 yards, 40 yards and 50 yards from the start marker.

Description
Wearing the parachute, the player accelerates to the 40-yard cone then decelerates.

Key teaching points
- Maintain correct running form/mechanics
- Do not worry if the wind and the resistance cause you to feel as though you are being pulled from side to side; this will in fact improve your balance and co-ordination
- Do not lean into the run too much
- Quality, not quantity is vital

Sets and reps
3 sets of 5 reps plus 1 contrast run with a walk-back recovery between each rep and 3 minutes recovery between each set.

Variations/progressions
- Explosive re-acceleration – the parachutes have a release mechanism; the player accelerates to the 30-yard cone where she releases the parachute and explodes to the 40-yard cone before decelerating
- Random change of direction – the coach stands behind the 30-yard cone; as the player releases the parachute the coach indicates a change in the direction of the run. When mastered, the coach can then introduce the ball for players to run on to during the explosive phase

DRILL BALL DROPS

Aim
To develop explosive reactions.

Area/equipment
Indoor or outdoor area; 1 or 2 balls.

Description
Work in pairs; Player 1 drops the ball at various distances and angles from her partner. The ball is dropped from shoulder height and immediately the partner explodes forward and attempts to catch or trap the ball before the second bounce. (Distances between players will differ because the height of the bounce will vary depending on the ground surface.)

Key teaching points
- Work off the balls of the feet – particularly prior to the drop
- Use a very explosive arm drive
- The initial steps should be short, fast and explosive
- At the take-off do not jump, stagger or hesitate
- Work on developing a smooth one-movement run

Sets and reps
3 sets of 10 reps with 2 minutes recovery between each set.

Variations/progressions
- Player to hold 2 balls and to drop just 1, so that partner anticipates and reacts to only 1 ball
- Work in groups of 3, with 2 of the players at different angles alternately dropping a ball for the third player to catch or trap. On achieving this, the player turns and accelerates away to catch/trap the second ball
- Alter the start positions, e.g. sideways, backwards with a call, seated, etc.

DRILL | *UPHILL RUNS*

Aim
To develop sprint endurance and explosive running.

Area/equipment
Outdoors. The hill should be about 20–40 yards long with a gradient of no more than 4%. A few cones can be used to mark out various distances.

Description
Players are to accelerate up the hill over the nominated distance and perform a slow jog back to the start position before repeating the drill.

Key teaching points
- Maintain correct running form/mechanics
- Ensure that strong knee and arm drives are used
- Work at maximal effort
- Adequate recovery time between reps is essential
- Do not attempt to run up hills with steep gradients as this will have a negative impact on the running mechanics

Sets and reps
3 sets of 6 reps with a jog-back recovery between reps and 3 minutes recovery between sets.

Variations/progressions
- Accelerate backwards over the initial few yards before turning to complete the drill as above
- Overspeed – accelerate down the hill; here control is vital!

DRILL — MEDICINE BALL (JELLY BALL) WORKOUT

Aim
To develop explosive upper-body and core power.

Area/equipment
Indoor or outdoor area; jelly balls of various weights from 5 to 20 lb.

Description
Working in pairs, the players perform simple throws, e.g. chest passes, single arm passes, front slams, back slams, twist passes, woodchopper and granny throws (*see* photos).

Key teaching points
- Start with a lighter ball for a warm-up set
- Start with simple movements first before progressing to twists etc.
- Keep the spine upright
- Take care when loading (catching) and unloading (throwing) as this can put stress on the lower back

Sets and reps
1 set of 12 reps of each drill with 1 minute recovery between each drill and 3 minutes recovery before the next exercise.

Variations/progressions
Long throw-ins – start by performing the throw-in with a normal ball, then throw a jelly ball for 6 reps before performing a contrast throw with a light foam or plastic ball and then with a soccer ball.

Chest pass

Front slam

Back slam

Woodchopper

Twist pass

DRILL *SLED RUNNING*

Aim
To develop explosive sprint endurance.

Area/equipment
Large outdoor grass area, cones and a Sprint Sled. Mark out an area 30–60 yards long.

Description
The player is connected to the sled and sprints over the nominated distance before recovering, turning around and repeating the drill.

Key teaching points
- Maintain correct running form/mechanics
- Maintain a strong arm drive
- Often players will need to use an exaggerated lean to initiate the momentum required to get the sled moving
- As momentum picks up, the player should take up the correct running position

Sets and reps
2 sets of 5 reps plus 1 contrast run with 1 minute recovery between each rep and 3 minutes recovery between each set.

Variations/progressions
5-yard explosive acceleration – the player covers 50 yards by alternating between acceleration and deceleration phases over distances of 5 yards.

DRILL   *PLYOMETRICS – LOW-IMPACT QUICK JUMPS*

Aim
To develop explosive power for running, jumping and changing direction.

Area/equipment
Indoor or outdoor area; Fast Foot Ladder, or cones placed at 18-inch intervals.

Description
The player performs double-footed single jumps – i.e. 1 jump between each rung (*see* fig. 5.7(a)). On reaching the end of the ladder, she turns round and jumps back.

Key teaching points
- Maintain correct jumping form/mechanics
- The emphasis is on the speed, *not* the height, of the jumps
- Start slowly and increase the speed but do not lose control, i.e. avoid feeling as though you are going to fall over the edge of a cliff when you reach the end of the drill

Sets and reps
2 sets of 2 reps with 1 minute recovery between each set.

Variations/progressions
- Backward jumps
- Two jumps forward and 1 back (*see* fig. 5.7(b))
- Sideways jumps
- Sideways jumps 2 forwards and 1 back
- Hopscotch – 2 feet inside then 2 feet outside the square
- Left- and right-footed hops
- Increase the intensity – replace ladders/cones with 7–12-inch hurdles and perform the drills detailed above

Key	
Direction of running	→
Player	X
Ladder	

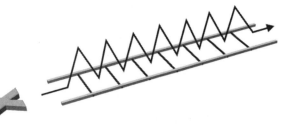

Figure 5.7(a) Low-impact, quick jumps

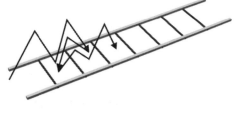

Figure 5.7(b) Low-impact, quick jumps – 2 forward and 1 back

DRILL   *PLYOMETRIC CIRCUIT*

Aim
To develop explosive multi-directional speed, agility and quickness.

Area/equipment
Indoor or outdoor area. Place ladders, hurdles and cones in a circuit formation (*see* fig. 5.8).

Description
The players are to jump, hop and zigzag their way through the circuit as stipulated by the coach.

Key teaching points
- Maintain the correct mechanics for each part of the circuit
- Ensure a smooth transfer from running to jumping movements and vice versa

Sets and reps
5 circuits with 1 minute recovery between each circuit.

Variations/progressions
Work in pairs, Player 1 completes the circuit while her partner feeds the ball at various points around the circuit, i.e. to head, chest or kick as necessary.

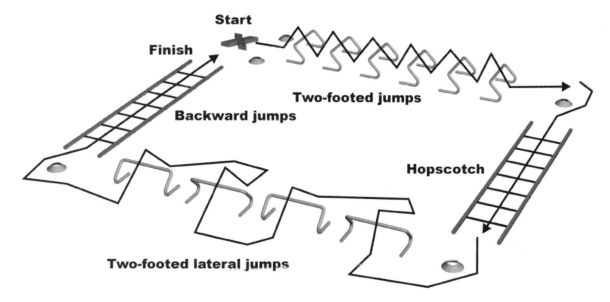

Figure 5.8 Plyometric circuit

DRILL DROP JUMPS

Aim
To develop explosive multi-directional speed.

Area/equipment
Indoor or outdoor area with a cushioned/grassed landing surface. A stable platform or bench to jump from of variable height – 15–36 inches depending on the stage in the season.

Description
The player stands on the platform, jumps off with her feet together, lands on the balls of the feet and then accelerates away for 5 yards.

Key teaching points
- Do not land flat-footed
- Do not sink into the hips on landing
- Maintain a strong core
- Keep the head up – this will help align the spine

Sets and reps
2 sets of 10 reps with 3 minutes recovery between each set.

Variations/progressions
- Backward drop jumps
- Side drop jumps
- Drop jumps with a mid-air twist
- Include a ball for the players to accelerate on to

CHAPTER 6 EXPRESSION OF POTENTIAL

TEAM GAMES IN PREPARATION FOR THE NEXT LEVEL

This stage is quite short in duration, but very important; players bring together all the elements of the continuum into a highly competitive situation involving other players.

Short, high-intensity 'tag'-type games and random agility tests work really well here. The key is to fire up the players to perform fast, explosive and controlled movements that leave them exhilarated, mentally and physically ready for the next stage of training, or the game on Saturday.

DRILL   'BRITISH BULLDOG'

Aim
To practise multi-directional explosive movements in a pressured situation.

Area/equipment
Outdoor or indoor area of approximately 20 square yards and about 20 cones to mark out start and finish lines.

Description
One player is nominated and stands in the centre of the grid, while the rest stand to one side (*see* fig. 6.1). On the coach's call all the players attempt to get to the opposite side of the square without being caught by the player in the middle. When the player in the middle captures another player, she then joins them in the middle and helps to capture more 'prisoners'.

Key teaching points
■ Use correct mechanics at all times
■ Keep head and eyes up to avoid collisions with other players

Sets and reps
Play British Bulldog for approximately 3–4 minutes before moving on to the more technical aspects of the game.

Variations/progressions
The player in the middle uses a soccer ball to touch other players in order to capture them.

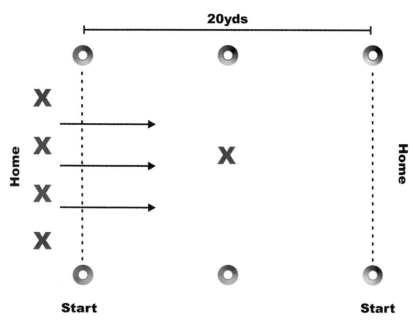

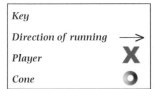

Figure 6.1 'British Bulldog'

DRILL CIRCLE BALL

Aim
To practise using explosive evasion skills.

Area/equipment
Outdoor or indoor area. Players make a circle about 15 yards in diameter (depending on the size of the squad).

Description
One or two players stand in the centre of the circle while the players on the outside have 1 or 2 balls (*see* fig. 6.2). The object is for those on the outside to try and make contact (with the ball) with those on the inside. The players on the inside try to dodge the balls. The winners are the pair who have the least number of hits during their time in the centre.

Key teaching points
Players on the inside should use the correct mechanics.

Sets and reps
Each pair to stay in the centre area for 45 seconds.

Variations/progressions
- Ball to be thrown *not* kicked
- Players in the middle have to hold on to each other

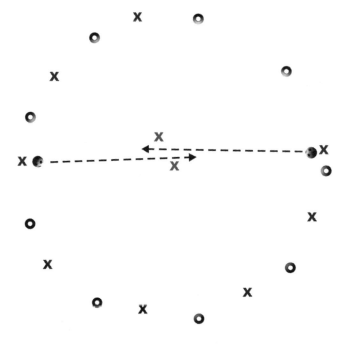

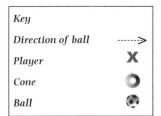

Key	
Direction of ball	------>
Player	**X**
Cone	◎
Ball	⚽

Figure 6.2 Circle ball

DRILL 'ROBBING THE NEST'

Aim
To practise multi-directional explosive speed, agility and quickness.

Area/equipment
Outdoor or indoor area of about 20 square yards, with a centre circle, measuring 2 yards in diameter, marked out with cones. Place a number of balls in the centre circle.

Description
Two nominated players protect the 'nest' of the balls with the rest of the players standing on the outside of the square area (*see* fig. 6.3). The game starts when the outside players run in and try to steal the footballs from the nest by dribbling to the outside of the square (safe zone). The two defenders of the nest try to prevent the robbers from getting the balls to the safe zone by stopping them with a fair tackle. For every successful tackle, the ball is returned to the centre circle.

Key teaching points
- Correct mechanics must be used at all times
- Players should dodge, swerve, weave, sidestep, etc.

Sets and reps
Each pair to defend for about 45 seconds.

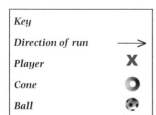

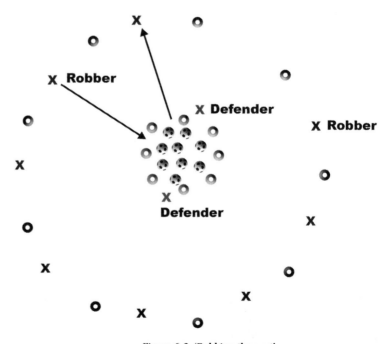

Figure 6.3 'Robbing the nest'

DRILL ODD ONE OUT

Aim
To practise speed, agility and quickness in a competitive environment.

Area/equipment
Outdoor or indoor area; cones and balls. Mark out a circle of 20–25 yards in diameter and a centre circle of about 2 yards in diameter.

Description
Place a number of balls in the centre area, one fewer than the number of players present. The players are situated on the outside of the larger circle (*see* fig. 6.4). On the coach's call the players start running round the larger circle. On the coach's second call they collect a ball from the centre circle as quickly as possible. The player without a ball is the odd man out and performs a soccer skill drill as directed by the coach. The coach then removes another ball and repeats the process.

Key teaching points
- Correct mechanics must be used at all times
- Players should be aware of other players around them

Sets and reps
Play the game until a winner emerges.

Variations/progressions
Work in pairs, i.e. one ball between two players.

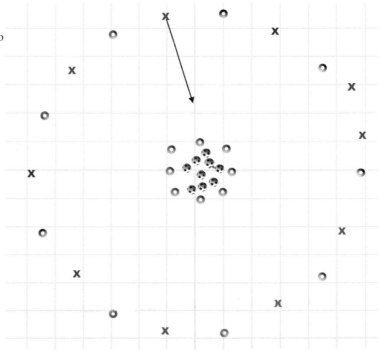

Key	
Direction of run	→
Player	**X**
Cone	◐
Ball	⚽

Figure 6.4 Odd one out

DRILL CONDITIONED GAMES – '2 TOUCH'

Aim
To practise speed, agility and quickness in competitive environments under specific conditions.

Area/equipment
Outdoor or indoor area adequate in size for the group being worked; cones and balls.

Description
The players are split into small teams (3 v. 3, 2 v. 2) the player in possession of the ball is allowed only 2 touches of the ball. The opponents' aim is to press, compete for and win the ball. Once in possession they are governed by the 2-touch rule.

Key teaching points
- Correct ball control and passing techniques must be used
- Good observation and communication are important
- Correct running techniques must be used when running off the ball

Sets and reps
Play for about 3–4 minutes.

Variations/progressions
- Play 1 touch
- Vary the number of players on each team, i.e. 3 v. 2, 3 v. 1
- Condition the type of pass, e.g. ball on the floor at all times

DRILL ■ CONE TURNS

Aim
To practise multi-directional speed, agility and quickness.

Area/equipment
Outdoor or indoor area of about 20 square yards; 50 small cone markers. Place the cones in and around the grid; 25 of the cones should be turned upside down.

Description
Working in two small teams (2–3 players), one team attempts to turn over the upright cones and the other team attempts to turn over the upside down cone (*see* fig. 6.5). The winners are the team that has the largest number of cones their way up after 60 seconds.

Key teaching points
■ Initiate good arm drive after turning a cone
■ Use correct multi-directional mechanics
■ Be aware of other players around the area

Sets and reps
A game should last for 60 seconds.

Variations/progressions
Use 4 teams and allocate 4 different-coloured cones.

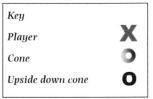

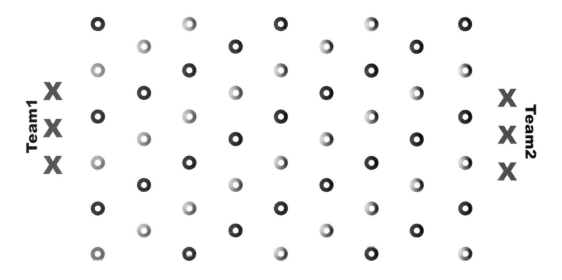

Figure 6.5 Cone turns

CHAPTER 7 POSITION–SPECIFIC DRILLS

In this chapter examples of position-specific patterns of movement are provided. By combining all areas of the SAQ Continuum including techniques, equipment and drills into game- and position-specific situations, you can improve and perfect the movement skills required by the players to succeed in these positions.

The primary aim is to improve the explosive speed, precision, control, power and co-ordination necessary for specific movements required by positions in all areas of the field. These are best introduced when the foundation work of SAQ has been mastered and during training sessions that are used to focus on positional techniques of individual players.

POSITION – WING BACK
DRILL ATTACKING WING BACK DRILL

Aim
To develop acceleration and speed of attack on the flanks, speed and control of deceleration. To develop the control and agility required to jockey backwards, turn and accelerate back to defend.

Area/equipment
For maximum impact the drill should be performed in the relevant position on the pitch; 3 Fast Foot Ladders, balls and cones (*see* fig. 7.1).

Description
The wing back accelerates down the first ladder and passes the ball that is at the end infield to a waiting player/coach. The player then accelerates over 30 yards to the start of the next ladder where she decelerates. On leaving the ladder, she crosses the ball that is at the end of the ladder into the opposition's box. The player then jockeys backwards for 10 yards (between the cones) keeping an eye on the result of the crossed ball before turning and accelerating through the third ladder and sprinting back to the start cone.

Key teaching points
- Concentrate on correct mechanics in all phases of sprinting including acceleration and deceleration
- Concentrate on the turn; this needs to be perfected, as poor turns can cost 2–3 yards
- Use correct techniques when on the ball
- Work both the left and right sides of the soccer pitch

Sets and reps
6 reps with 2 minutes recovery between each rep.

Variations/progressions
- Work in pairs with one player feeding the ball in at various stages throughout the drill
- Place cones in the first extended sprint area for swerves and zigzags

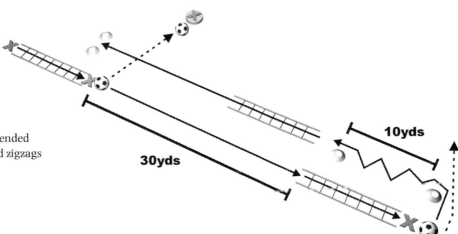

Figure 7.1 Attacking wing-back drill

DRILL   *PRESS AND JOCKEY BACKWARDS*

Aim

To develop players' ability to press or close down an opponent and then successfully maintain pressure on her while jockeying backwards.

Area/equipment

For maximum impact the drill should be performed in the relevant position on the pitch. Set out 1 short Fast Foot Ladder and cones as shown in fig. 7.2.

Description

Player 1 stands to the right of the ladder and accelerates straight to the cone A. The player continues to face in the same direction as they move across and perform the icky shuffle backwards through the ladder.

Key teaching points

- Maintain correct running form/mechanics
- Keep looking up and ahead when performing the icky shuffle
- Work off the balls of the feet

Sets and reps

2 sets of 10 reps (5 starting on the right and 5 on the left) with 15 seconds recovery between reps and 2 minutes recovery between each set.

Variations/progressions

- On reaching cone A or B receive and return a ball that has been delivered in by the coach
- Vary the players' initial starting positions to encourage turning and accelerating away

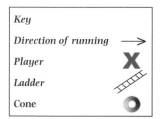

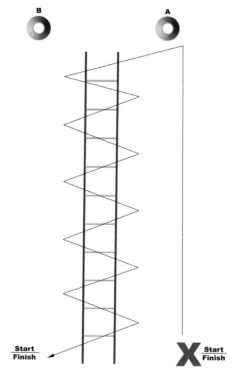

Figure 7.2 Press and jockey backwards

POSITION – ALL DEFENDERS

DRILL *PRESSING A CLEARED BALL*

Aim

To develop players' ability to defend the ball when it has been cleared from a dangerous position. This can be from crosses, set pieces and shots that require clearing the ball quickly. To develop players' understanding of the need to press and close down the space between themselves and the ball.

Area/equipment

For maximum impact the drill should be performed in the relevant position on the pitch. Hand weights and 8 cones set out in a grid (*see* fig. 7.3).

Description

The defender starts in a position between cones A and B holding the hand weights. The coach calls the player to move forwards and backwards between the 2 cones. The coach then nominates 1 of the 6 outfield cones that represents where the ball has been cleared to. The player turns, accelerates and after the first 4/5 steps drops the weights then explodes to the cone. On completion of the drill the player jogs back to the starting position.

Key teaching points

■ Maintain correct running form/mechanics
■ Use short steps and a strong arm drive when turning and accelerating
■ Hand weights to be dropped as part of the running technique; do not stop or allow the arm mechanics to falter

Sets and reps

3 sets of 5 reps plus 1 contrast run with 2 minutes recovery between each set.

Variations/progressions

■ Introduce jumping for the ball prior to the acceleration phase
■ Remove the outfield cones and replace with players; each player is to have a ball and the defender presses the nominated player who takes the defender on

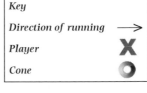

Key
Direction of running →
Player **X**
Cone **O**

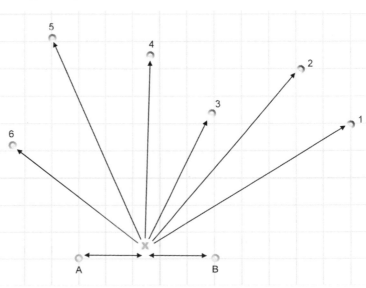

Figure 7.3 Pressing a cleared ball

POSITION – ALL DEFENDERS
DRILL CUTTING ACROSS THE OPPONENT

Aim

A primary concern for a defender in front of goal is to get in front of and across the attacking opponent and to cut off their ball supply. This drill develops the skill with controlled explosion.

Area/equipment

For maximum impact the drill should be performed in the relevant position on the pitch. Set out ball and cones as in fig. 7.4(a); Viper Belt with 2 Flexi-cords attached, one to each side.

Description

Work in groups of 4 with Player 1 wearing the Viper Belt; Player 2 holds a Flexi-cord and stands directly behind Player 1. Player 3 holds the other Flexi-cord and stands to either the left or right of Player 1. The fourth player stands further down the grid ready to deliver a ball (*see* fig. 7.4(b)). Player 1 accelerates down the grid, Player 2 stands still and provides a resistance, Player 3 runs laterally in line with Player 1. When Player 1 reaches the area between cone A and B she sidesteps towards cone D. Meanwhile, Player 3 stands still at cone C to provide a lateral resistance. On reaching cone D, Player 1 receives a ball delivered by Player 4 that she heads, chests or side-foots back. Player 1 then jockeys back to the starting position.

Key teaching points

- Maintain correct running form/mechanics
- When moving laterally do not skip, sink into the hips or allow the feet to cross
- Use small steps when moving laterally

Sets and reps

2 sets of 8 reps (4 moving to the left and 4 to the right) plus 1 contrast run with 2 minutes recovery between each set.

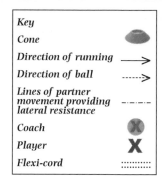

Key

Cone	
Direction of running	→
Direction of ball	---→
Lines of partner movement providing lateral resistance	-·-·-·-
Coach	(X)
Player	X
Flexi-cord	·········

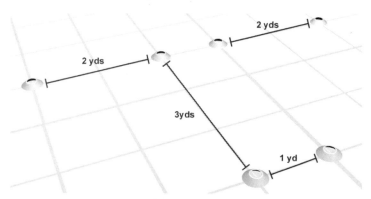

Figure 7.4(a) Cutting across opponent (grid)

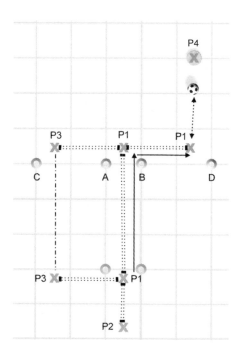

Figure 7.4(b) Cutting across opponent (drill)

POSITION – MIDFIELDERS

DRILL **PALMER DRILL**

Aim
To develop speed, agility and control in a progressive centre-field pressing drill – the object is to cut off attacking moves through the heart of the defence.

Area/equipment
For maximum impact the drill should be performed in the relevant position on the pitch. Place 2 Fast Foot Ladders and cones in the formation shown in the fig. 7.5.

Description
The player accelerates down the ladder and moves explosively at the appropriate angle to the cone indicated by the coach. Having reached the cone the player jockeys backwards to the start/finish line.

Key teaching points
- Maintain correct running form/mechanics
- Develop awareness through the ladders by looking up
- Maintain an explosive arm drive during the change in direction phase
- Work both to left and right of the ladder

Sets and reps
1 set of 8 reps (coach should try to call 4 to the left and 4 to the right) with 15 seconds recovery between reps.

Variations/progressions
This variation involves the second ladder. The aim of this drill is to develop the centre half's explosive speed to close down an attacker who has decelerated early to draw the centre half out of defence. The timing is crucial! The centre half player accelerates down the first ladder and then sprints to the second ladder and decelerates down this ladder. On leaving the second ladder, the player moves explosively at the appropriate angle to the nominated cone, jockeys backwards for a few yards, turns and accelerates back to the start/finish line.

Key

Direction of running	→
Player	X
Cone	⬭
Ladder	▱
Jockey backwards	∿

Variation 1 progression

Drill variation 1

10 yds

Start/finish

Figure 7.5 Palmer drill

POSITION – MIDFIELDERS

DRILL BACKWARD TURN AND COVER

Aim

Teams may tactically attempt to bypass the midfield players by using the ball over the top. This requires the defensive midfielder to anticipate the direction of the pass by keeping an eye on the ball while covering backwards. When the pass is delivered, the player is required to turn, accelerate and cover. The speed of the turn and acceleration to cover is crucial!

Area/equipment

For maximum impact the drill should be performed in the relevant position on the pitch; use 9 cones and a Viper Belt with a leash attachment (if you do not have a Viper Belt and leash, you can use a towel around the player's waist). Place the cones in a fan formation (*see* fig. 7.6).

Description

Work in pairs with Player 1 wearing the Viper Belt and Player 2 providing resistance by holding the leash attachment. Player 1 faces Player 2 and moves backwards to an inner nominated cone. Player 2 provides some resistance but does go with Player 1. On arriving at the cone, the leash is released by Player 2. Player 1 explodes in to a turn and sprints to a nominated outer cone.

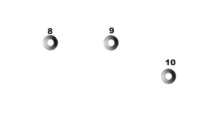

Key	
Cone	⊙
Direction of running	⟶
Player	**X**
Flexi-cord	··········

Key teaching points

■ Maintain an upright position while moving backwards
■ Use a strong arm drive while moving backwards
■ On the turn, keep the feet shoulder-width apart; do not allow the feet to cross over
■ After the turn as the player comes into the linear position she should adopt an upright sprinting posture as soon as possible
■ Player 2 should use short steps

Sets and reps

1 set of 6 reps with a walk-back recovery between each rep and 3 minutes recovery before starting the next exercise.

Variations/progressions

■ On the release, the coach can deliver a ball to an outer marker, the player must explode to the ball and retrieve it
■ A player with the ball is moving between the outside cones, on the coach's call Player 1 turns, explodes and initiates a tackle on the player with the ball, whose aim is to beat Player 1

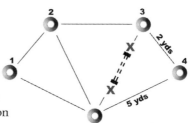

Figure 7.6 Backward turn and cover

POSITION – ATTACKING MIDFIELDERS

DRILL *TURN AND ATTACK*

Aim
To develop explosive precise turn and chase skills. Midfielders often face their own goal waiting for the ball to be cleared by the defender or the goalkeeper. On many occasions the ball will go over the midfielder who will turn explosively, chase and regain the ball before setting up an attacking opportunity.

Area/equipment
For maximum impact the drill should be performed in the relevant position on the pitch; use hand weights and cones set up in a Y formation (*see* fig. 7.7).

Description
The midfielder holding the hand weights runs backwards for 5 yards and without slowing down or changing mechanics turns either to the left or right, explodes to the first set of cones where the hand weights are released to allow the player to explode again to the outside cones.

Key teaching points
- Maintain correct mechanics when running backwards, turning and running forwards
- Increase the arm drive during the turn and acceleration phase
- Work off the balls of the feet, particularly when working backwards
- Release the arms without stopping or interrupting the arm mechanics

Sets and reps
2 sets of 6 reps with a walk-back recovery between each rep and 2 minutes recovery between each set.

Variations/progressions
Get the midfielder to work sideways for the first 5 yards then turn and explode. Ensure that the sideways foot movements are short steps and not skips.

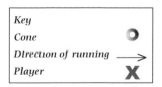

Key	
Cone	⦿
Direction of running	→
Player	**X**

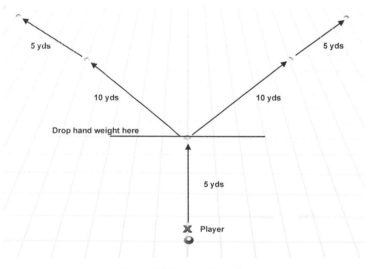

5 yds   5 yds

10 yds   10 yds

Drop hand weight here

5 yds

X Player

Figure 7.7 Turn and attack

POSITION – MIDFIELDERS

| DRILL | BALL CONTROL, FEED, TURN, RECEIVE, SHOOT |

Aim

To develop explosive turn and running skills. Midfielders often receive the ball while they are facing their own goal and they use either their head, chest or foot to control the ball before quickly feeding it to a support player. The midfielder then turns and moves off at an angle to make herself available for the return pass so as to shoot at goal from 20–25 yards.

Area/equipment

For maximum impact the drill should be performed in the relevant position on the pitch; use hand weights and cones placed as shown in fig. 7.8.

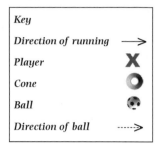

Key	
Direction of running	→
Player	X
Cone	◉
Ball	⚽
Direction of ball	⇢

Description

Work in pairs. Player 1 holds the hand weights and accelerates towards the centre cone B. Player 2 at cone C delivers the ball to Player 1. Player 2 then moves off on an arcing run around either cone D or E. Player 1 on receiving the ball lays it off into the path of Player 2's arcing run. Player 1 then turns explosively and accelerates down the centre of the grid towards the goal/cones. After 5 yards, Player 1 releases the weights, Player 2 passes into the path of Player 1 who explodes on to the ball and drives it into the goal.

Key teaching points

- Maintain correct mechanics in all directional running
- Player 2 should use a powerful arm drive when making the arcing run – this helps control
- Player 1 should use explosive arm drive during the turn phase and must not allow the feet to cross
- Players should communicate verbally and visually

Sets and reps

1 set of 8 reps with a walk-back recovery between each rep.

Variations/progressions

- Player 1 commences the drill by moving sideways for the first 5 yards
- Player 2 also uses light hand weights that are dropped halfway through the arced run

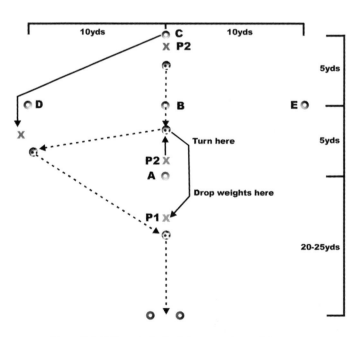

Figure 7.8 Ball control – feed, turn, receive and shoot

POSITION – MIDFIELDERS

DRILL *LATERAL LUNGES WITH THE BALL*

Aim

To develop explosive co-ordinated lateral lunges with ball control. Midfielders are often required to perform well-timed lateral lunges as well as to be able to control and pass the ball while moving laterally.

Area/equipment

Indoor or outdoor area of approx. 20 square yards. Lay out one 15-foot section of ladder, 4 cones and 3 agility poles (*see* fig. 7.9); footballs.

Description

The player starts on one side of the ladder, steps across and into the ladder and then uses a sidestep lunge across and out of the ladder towards the first pole. The player returns to the cone-free space in the ladder before moving laterally out of the other side to volley a ball that has been delivered by the coach. The drill is repeated for the length of the ladder before the player walks back to the start position.

Key teaching points

- Use a strong arm drive to assist lateral movement, balance and agility
- Use correct soccer techniques
- Use short steps through the ladder
- Maintain a strong core and posture

Sets and reps

3 sets of 6 reps (3 reps lunging to the left and 3 to the right) with a walk-back recovery between reps and 2 minutes recovery between sets.

Variations/progressions

- Perform the drill backwards
- Vary the ball skill, e.g. head and chest the ball, volley, etc.

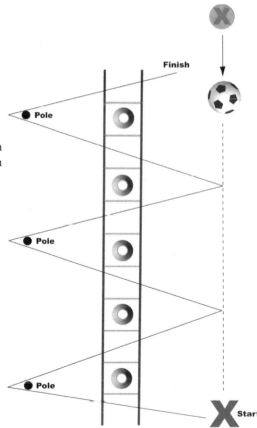

Figure 7.9 Lateral lunges with the ball

POSITION – MIDFIELDERS

DRILL ASSISTED/RESISTED ARCING AND ANGLED RUN

Aim

To develop timed, explosive arced runs in to the defensive area. Attacking midfielders who run well-timed, angled or arced runs in and around the penalty area are very difficult for defenders to pick up.

Area/equipment

For maximum impact the drill should be performed in the relevant position on the pitch; use 2 Viper Belts, Flexi-cord and cones. Place a cone every 2 yards in an arc shape that is about 20 yards long. Make several arcs and vary their directions and angles. (These should also vary from session to session.)

Description

Work in pairs. Both players wear Viper Belts and are attached to one another by a Flexi-cord so that the lead runner is resisted from behind and the back runner is assisted by the lead runner. Standing at the start the lead runner sets off; the Flexi-cord will stretch after about 4–5 yards, and then the back runner sets off.

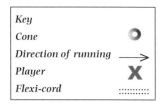

Key	
Cone	◎
Direction of running	→
Player	**X**
Flexi-cord	··········

Key teaching points

▪ Both players should maintain correct running form/mechanics
▪ Assisted player should lean into the assistance – do not lean back
▪ Do not stretch the Flexi-cord more than 3 times its normal length
▪ Alternate players between lead and back runner after each run
▪ Always finish a set with contrast runs

Sets and reps

1 set of 8 reps, i.e. 4 lead runs for each player with 90 seconds recovery between each rep and 3 minutes before the next exercise.

Variations/progressions

The lead runner runs backwards and turns after the back runner has started her explosive phase.

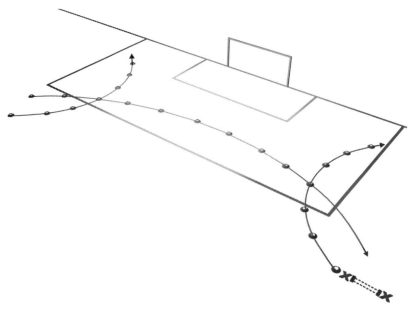

Figure 7.10 Assisted and resisted arcing and angled runs

POSITION – ATTACKING MIDFIELDERS

DRILL | *OVERSPEED ARC RUNNING*

Aim

One of the best weapons for an attacking midfielder is the ability to run on explosive arcs into the penalty area. This makes the player difficult to stop and defend against.

Area/equipment

For maximum impact the drill should be performed in the relevant position on the pitch. Use an Overspeed Tow Rope, and set out cones to make arcs of about 40 yards long starting in the midfield and ending up somewhere in the penalty box.

Description

Players 1 and 2 are attached by the Overspeed Tow Rope belts. Player 1 is assisted from the front and Player 2 is resisted from the back. Player 3 holds the handle and provides different levels of overspeed. Player 1 will run the arc, Player 2 runs in a straight line away from Player 3 who moves back towards the original start point of Player 1. Player 3 must simultaneously keep an eye on Player 1 to ensure that the right level of assistance is being provided.

Key teaching points

- Players 1 and 2 must use correct running form/mechanics
- Player 1 must relax and must not resist the power
- Player 1 should lean slightly into the pull, *not* against it
- Player 2 should take short fast steps – do not sink into the hips
- Player 3 must keep an eye on Player 1 – do not overload the power

Sets and reps

After 1 rep, rotate the players:

the resisted player becomes assisted, assisted becomes Player 3/control and Player 3/control becomes the resisted player. Each player is to perform 5 reps.

Variations/progressions

Advanced – Player 1 swerves in and out of some cones while running the arc.

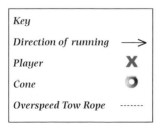

Key

Direction of running	⟶
Player	X
Cone	◎
Overspeed Tow Rope	-------

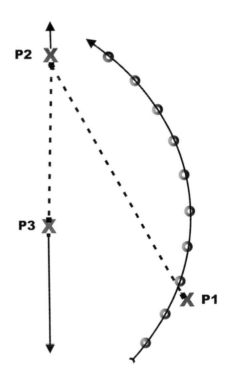

Figure 7.11 Overspeed arc running

121

POSITION – FORWARDS
DRILL PEEL OFF AND TURN

Aim

Forwards have less space to work in, particularly when they are close to goal. The difference between scoring and missing can be a matter of inches, so all forwards need to be multi-directionally explosive over the first 3–5 yards. This drill will help to develop the movements required when a player has her back to the goal and is closely marked. The player peels off quickly to get into the space vacated by the defender to receive a pass and shoot for goal.

Area/equipment

For maximum impact the drill should be performed in the relevant position on the pitch; use a Viper Belt, Flexi-cord and 3 cones marked out in a line 8 yards long (*see* fig. 7.12) with a centre cone 4 yards away from the start.

Description

Player 1 wears the Viper Belt loosely to allow her to turn within the belt, and stands on cone B. Player 2 holds the Flexi-cord on cone A. Player 1 accelerates explosively towards cone C then swivels in the belt to explode back to cone A.

Key teaching points

- Use an explosive arm drive
- Use short explosive steps during the turn
- After the turn, lean into the assistance, do not lean back

Sets and reps

2 sets of 6 reps plus 1 contrast run with a walk-back recovery between reps and 3 minutes recovery between sets.

Variations/progressions

Player 2 has a ball and passes to Player 1 as she explodes back towards cone A.

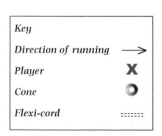

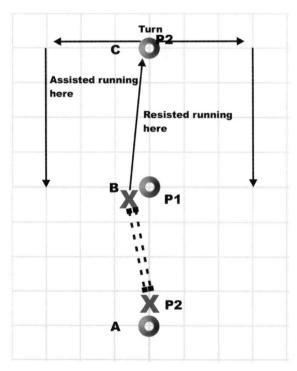

Figure 7.12 Peel off and turn

DRILL ACCELERATION/DECELERATION STRIDE DRILL

Aim

To develop explosive acceleration, controlled stride frequency, deceleration and change of direction in a game-like situation.

Area/equipment

For maximum impact the drill should be performed in the relevant position on the pitch; use 2 mannequins, stride frequency canes and balls placed as shown in fig. 7.13.

Description

Player 1 accelerates towards mannequin A and cuts out to the side of the mannequin away from the stride frequency canes. At this point coach X feeds a ball in for Player 1 to volley back. Player 1 then cuts back inside the mannequin and accelerates down the stride canes. On reaching the end cane, Player 1 repeats the earlier movement around mannequin B. Having volleyed the ball back, Player 1 cuts inside mannequin B and accelerates away for 5 yards.

Key teaching points

- Take small strides in the acceleration, deceleration and change of lateral direction phases
- Maintain correct mechanics in all directional running
- Work off the balls of the feet
- Apply good soccer techniques

Sets and reps

1 set of 6 reps with a walk-back recovery between reps.

Variations/progressions

- Vary the soccer skill
- Replace mannequin A with Player 2 who supports the run of Player 1 and performs a passing drill from coach Y's feed

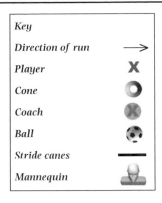

Key

Direction of run	→
Player	X
Cone	◉
Coach	⊗
Ball	⚽
Stride canes	—
Mannequin	🔲

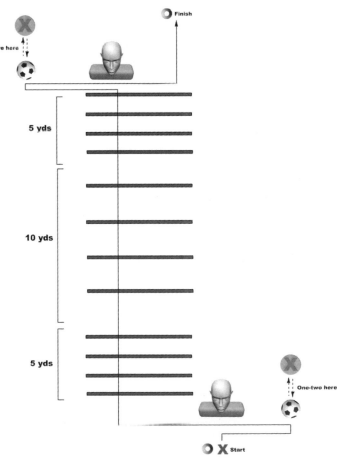

Figure 7.13 Acceleration/deceleration stride drill with ball

POSITION – FORWARDS

DRILL CROSS AND ATTACK GOAL

Aim

To develop short, explosive angled movements. Many forwards score goals by moving parallel to the goal then darting in through a gap to strike or head a ball crossed over the face of the goal. Sometimes only the tiniest of touches is required to put the ball in the net. This drill has been developed to add explosion to the initial sideways and backwards movements that are used to confuse the defence and the explosive darting movement through a gap to contact the ball.

Area/equipment

For maximum impact the drill should be performed in the relevant position on the pitch; use a Viper Belt with 2 Flexi-cords attached front and back and 2 cones placed 7 yards apart on the 6-yard line in front of the goal. The other 5 cones are placed 2 yards away and in a straight line (*see* fig. 7.14).

Description

Work in groups of 3. Player 1 wears the Viper Belt with a Flexi-cord attached at the front that is held by Player 2. The second Flexi-cord is attached at the back and held by Player 3. Player 1 stands between the 2 cones on the 6-yard line with Players 2 and 3 standing on cones A and B respectively. On the coach's call Player 1 explodes the 2 yards to a nominated cone and then returns gently back to the start position for the next rep.

Key teaching points

- Work off the balls of the feet
- On the coach's call use an explosive arm drive
- The initial steps should be kept short, precise and explosive
- The feet should be kept shoulder-width apart as much as possible. This is crucial just in case the player has to jump to contact the ball

Sets and reps

1 set of 8 reps plus 1 contrast run with a walk-back recovery between reps and 3 minutes recovery before the next exercise.

Variations/progressions

- Vary Player 1's starting position
- Use a fourth player who nominates a cone for Player 1 to explode to before feeding the ball at different angles and heights for Player 1 to strike at goal

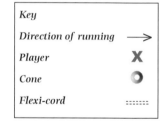

Key	
Direction of running	⟶
Player	X
Cone	◖
Flexi-cord	::::::::

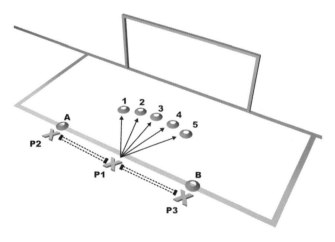

Figure 7.14 Moving across and attacking the goal mouth

DRILL *VERTICAL EXPLOSIVE HEADING POWER*

Aim
To develop the ability of the centre forward to explode as high as possible to meet the crosses and direct them towards the goal.

Area/equipment
For maximum impact the drill should be performed in the relevant position on the pitch. Use a Viper Belt with 3 Flexi-cords (1 attached to each of the 3 anchor points) and 2 cones placed 7 yards apart in front of goal on the 6-yard line.

Description
Player 1 (centre forward) wears the Viper Belt and stands in a central position between cones A and B. Player 2 holds a Flexi-cord on cone A and Player 3 likewise at cone B. Player 4 has the third Flexi-cord which is attached to the back of the Viper Belt and stands about 4 yards away from Player 1 outside the 6-yard area (near the penalty spot). The coach throws the ball at different heights between Player 1 and the goal line for her to head into the goal. Player 1 returns to the start position after each rep.

Key teaching points
- Use explosive jump mechanics, especially arms for the take off
- Players 2, 3 and 4 should remain seated on the ground for the duration of the drill to increase the resistance
- Player 1 must not sink into the hips on landing
- Player 1 should try to stay upright and on the balls of the feet at all times

Key	
Direction of running	$\longrightarrow$
Direction of ball	$\dashrightarrow$
Player	**X**
Coach	
Cone	
Flexi-cord	········

Sets and reps
1 set of 10 reps plus 2 contrast drills with a walk-back recovery between reps and 3 minutes before the next exercise.

Variations/progressions
Introduce defenders in front of Player 1 to create a competitive jump/heading situation.

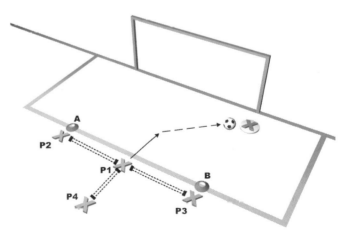

Figure 7.15 Vertical explosive heading power

SAQ Training for goalkeepers

Recent research highlights the importance of specific conditioning being incorporated as a regular feature of a goalkeeper's training programme.

Relying on standard training methods used by other outfield players neglects to consider the specialist and specific conditioning required by goalkeepers. The demands placed on the goalkeeper are quite different from those placed on the outfield players. The ability to utilise the stretch and shortening cycle (*see* page 00) will have a positive impact on the explosive motion required while diving and springing into action.

Match analysis investigating the demands placed upon goalkeepers highlighted the following:

- 86% of playing time was spent walking or standing still.

- The remaining 14% – the equivalent of 12 minutes – required the goalkeepers to make on average 13 saves or intercept crosses and 23 short 4–5 yard sprints.

- Many of the movements forwards, backwards and sideways indicated that a high level of multi-directional speed and agility were required.

Additional results indicate that most goals are conceded in the second half or after periods of high-intensity work when the goalkeeper's explosive abilities have been fatigued.

The ability of the goalkeeper to be explosive and multi-directional throughout the game is crucial. The flying dive to the bottom corner to fingertip the ball around the post is vital not only in the first but also in the last minute of the game. In the English Premiership, almost 70% of goals are scored in the bottom corners.

The following drills have been designed to ensure that goalkeepers become and remain explosive throughout the game.

POSITION – GOALKEEPER

DRILL NARROWING THE ANGLES

Aim

To develop explosive acceleration and speed, balance and agility over the first 5–10 yards. To assist the goalkeeper in narrowing the angle of players' runs towards the goal and to cut out through passes.

Area/equipment

For maximum impact the drill should be performed in the relevant position on the pitch. Use 4 short ladders and 7–8 cones. Place the 4 ladders just inside the 6-yard area (*see* fig. 7.16(a)) and the cones at different angles and distances of 5, 10 and 15 yards away from the ends of the ladders.

Description

The coach nominates which ladder (A, B ,C or D) the goalkeeper is to run down and which cone (1–8) she is to attack. The goalkeeper explodes down the ladder then angles off and accelerates to the nominated cone where she sets herself for the save or dive.

Key teaching points

- The initial steps should be short and explosive
- Maintain a powerful arm drive
- Keep the head and eyes up
- Just before reaching the cone, the goalkeeper should extend her arms and make herself look big

Sets and reps

2 set of 6 reps with a walk-back recovery between each rep and 3 minutes recovery between each set.

Variations/progressions

- Introduce a ball
- Replace the cones with 1 or 2 players who move back and forth across the penalty area. The coach nominates the ladder for the goalkeeper to explode down, who then attempts to stop the outfield player who has just started their attack on goal
- The goalkeeper wears a Viper Belt attached to a partner who works with the goalkeeper but creates a resistance throughout the drill
- Place 6 short ladders in a semi-circle around the goalkeeper and repeat the drill (*see* fig. 7.16(b))

Key	
Direction of running	$\longrightarrow$
Goalkeeper	**X**
Cone	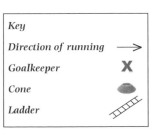
Ladder	

NARROWING THE ANGLES cont.

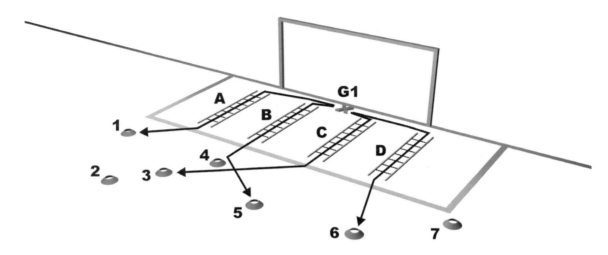

Figure 7.16(a) Explosive acceleration, narrowing the angles

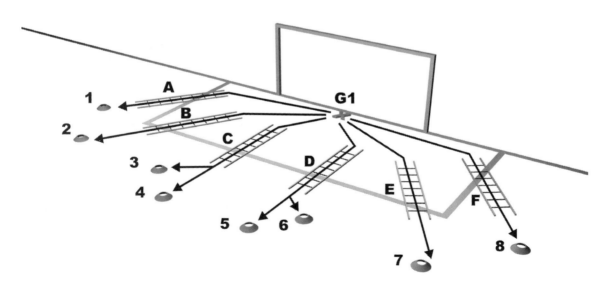

Figure 7.16(b) Explosive acceleration, narrowing the angles – variation

POSITION – GOALKEEPER

DRILL   *LATERAL SPEED DEVELOPMENT*

Aim

To develop fast controlled lateral movement across the goalmouth making the goalkeeper difficult to get past and thus cutting down the options for the attacking players.

Area/equipment

For maximum impact the drill should be performed in the relevant position on the pitch. Use 2 ladders and 6 balls; place the ladders just in front of the goal line leaving a small space between them where the goalkeeper will stand (*see* fig. 7.17). Place the balls on a line parallel with the ladders approximately 1 yard away.

Description

The goalkeeper stands between the 2 ladders and on the coach's call commences lateral fast-foot drills to either the left or right. The coach then nominates a ball (1, 2 or 3) and the goalkeeper explodes out of the ladder and on to the ball.

Key teaching points

- Stay tall during the lateral drills
- Use a few quick arm drives then revert to a 'ready' position i.e. extended arms and hands as if to save the ball
- Keep the head and eyes up

Sets and reps

2 set of 6 reps with a walk-back recovery between each rep and 3 minutes recovery between each set.

Variations/progressions

- Position 2 players just outside the 6-yard area, 1 on each side. On the coach's call the goalkeeper and the player both attack the same ball
- The goalkeeper wears a Viper Belt with 2 Flexi-cords attached to players standing on either side of the goal in order to work under resistance

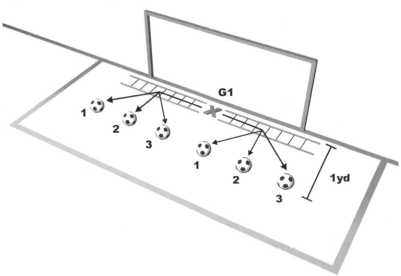

Figure 7.17 Lateral speed development

POSITION – GOALKEEPER
DRILL EXPLOSIVE DIVING

Aim

To develop multi-directional explosive diving – making the goalkeeper virtually unbeatable.

Area/equipment

For maximum impact the drill should be performed in the relevant position on the pitch. Use balls and a Viper Belt with 2 Flexi-cords attached, one either side. The other end of the Flexi-cord should be attached to either goalpost at waist height.

Description

The goalkeeper wears the belt and stands in the centre of the goal. The coach stands with the balls in the centre of the 6-yard line; she then sends the balls towards the goal at different angles and heights. The goalkeeper attempts to save these by moving explosively in the appropriate direction before recovering, resuming position before repeating the drill.

Key teaching points

- The goalkeeper should use short, explosive steps
- Do not sink into the hips
- Stay tall and 'big'
- Keep the head and eyes up
- Work off the balls of the feet at all times
- Keep the shoulders relaxed

Sets and reps

2 sets of 10 reps plus 2 contrast saves with a walk-back recovery between each rep and 3 minutes recovery between each set.

Variations/progressions

Introduce 2 saves per repetition.

Key	
Direction of running	→
Goalkeeper	X
Coach	
Ball	●
Flexi-cord	┈┈┈

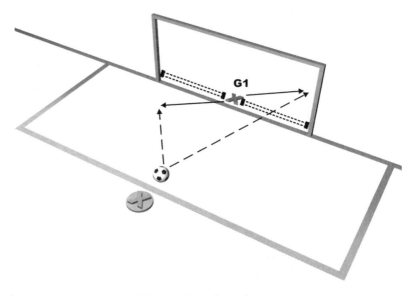

Figure 7.18 Explosive diving

DRILL

POSITION – GOALKEEPER
ACCELERATION AND JUMP DRILL

Aim

To develop explosive speed over a short distance and an explosive vertical jump. The ability to do this will allow the goalkeeper to cut down space in danger areas and control balls crossed and floated into this area.

Area/equipment

For maximum impact the drill should be performed in the relevant position on the pitch. Use a Viper Belt with 2 Flexi-cords attached, one on either side, and 6 cones. Place 2 starting cones (A and B) 3 yards away from the goal line (*see* fig. 7.19). The remaining 4 cones are placed 3–4 yards away, i.e. on or just over the 6-yard line, at different angles.

Description

Goalkeeper 1 wears the Viper Belt and Goalkeeper 2 stands behind the goal line holding both the Flexi-cords. The coach then nominates a cone and Goalkeeper 1 accelerates towards it; on reaching the cone Goalkeeper 1 either dives or jumps into the air. On landing, Goalkeeper 1 jockeys quickly back to the start position to await the next instruction.

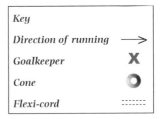

Key	
Direction of running	$\longrightarrow$
Goalkeeper	**X**
Cone	◉
Flexi-cord	┄┄┄

Key teaching points

- The goalkeeper should use short and explosive steps
- Goalkeeper 1 should stay tall
- Goalkeeper 1 should keep the head and eyes up
- Goalkeeper 2 should remain in a static, crouched position to increase the level of resistance

Sets and reps

2 set of 10 reps plus 2 contrast runs with the backwards jockey as the recovery between each rep and 3 minutes recovery between each set.

Variations/progressions

- Work the goalkeeper laterally by turning the belt around and working sideways onto the cones; the goalkeeper should use short, sharp steps, not skips
- At the nominated cone the goalkeeper is to make 2 saves (1 high and 1 low) before jockeying backwards to the start position

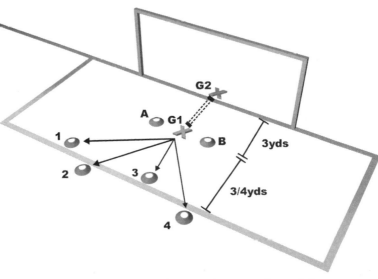

Figure 7.19 Resisted explosive acceleration and jump drill

POSITION – GOALKEEPER
DRILL EXPLOSIVE GROUND REACTION

Aim

To develop explosive 'get-ups' for goalkeepers who have just performed a save, are on the ground and have to get up as quickly as possible to perform another save or block.

Area/equipment

For maximum impact the drill should be performed in the relevant position on the pitch. Use jelly balls and various weights depending on the age group. Seniors should use 5–7 kg balls.

Description

The goalkeeper lies on her back holding the jelly ball to her chest. On a call from the coach the goalkeeper simultaneously gets up and throws the jelly ball away, finishing the drill in a ready position.

Key teaching points

- Try to make the get-up one continuous movement
- Try to get onto the balls of the feet as quickly as possible

Sets and reps

3 set of 10 reps plus 1 contrast without the jelly ball with the return to the start position as the recovery between reps and 3 minutes recovery between each set.

Variations/progressions

- Vary the start position, i.e. side, knees, turn, etc.
- Introduce a football for the goalkeeper to save as soon as she has got to her feet
- The goalkeeper is to sit on an agility disc with the ball held to her chest, repeat the drill as above

DRILL ***POSITION – GOALKEEPER***
EYE–HAND REACTION

Aim

To develop fast, accurate catching skills. To develop the goalkeeper's visual skills in following the ball in flight.

Area/equipment

Outdoor or indoor area. Use a Visual Acuity Ring.

Description

Work in pairs approximately 5 yards apart. The ring is tossed so that it rotates through the air and is caught by the goalkeeper on the colour nominated by the coach.

Key teaching points

■ Keep the head still – move the eyes to track the ring
■ Work off the balls of the feet at all times
■ The hands should be out and in front of the body ready to catch the ring

Sets and reps

2 sets of 20 reps with 1 minute recovery between each set.

Variations/progressions

Turn and catch.

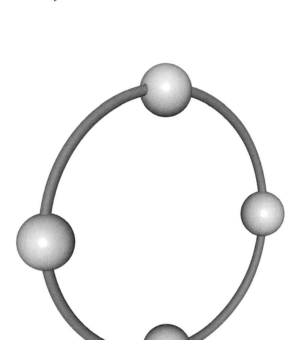

Figure 7.20 Visual Acuity Ring

POSITION – GOALKEEPER

DRILL PERIPHERAL AWARENESS

Aim
To develop peripheral awareness: to help the goalkeeper detect and react to the ball coming from behind and from the side more quickly.

Area/equipment
Outdoor or indoor area; use a Peripheral Vision Stick.

Description
Work in pairs with 1 player behind the goalkeeper who stands in a ready position. The player holds the stick and moves it from behind the goalkeeper into her field of vision. As soon as the goalkeeper detects the stick she claps both hands over the ball at the end of the stick.

Key teaching points
- The goalkeeper should work off the balls of the feet and in a slightly crouched position with the hands held out ready
- The player must be careful not to touch any part of the goalkeeper's body with the stick
- The player should vary the speed at which the stick is brought into the goalkeeper's field of vision

Sets and reps
2 set of 20 reps with no recovery between each rep and 1 minute recovery between each set.

Variations/progressions
Instead of using a vision stick, throw balls from behind the goalkeeper that they have to fend them off.

Figure 7.21 Peripheral Vision Stick

POSITION – GOALKEEPER

DRILL *EXPLOSIVE HAND/ARM REACTION*

Aim

To develop explosive reactions of the upper limbs that are crucial for goalkeepers to perform lightning-quick saves.

Area/equipment

For maximum impact the drill should be performed in the relevant position on the pitch, i.e. in the goal. Use balls and a Side-Stepper.

Description

The goalkeeper wears the Side-Stepper around her wrists and the coach stands 3–4 yards away with a bag of balls, feeding them in so that they are within an arm's length of the goalkeeper. The goalkeeper makes the save with one arm or hand and holds the other hand to the middle of her chest – that provides the required resistance.

Key teaching points

- Always perform the contrast immediately after the set is complete
- Work off the balls of the feet
- Goalkeepers must be given sufficient time to get set before each save is attempted
- Ensure that the ball is fed in to both sides

Sets and reps

3 sets of 10 reps plus 2 contrasts with 2 minutes recovery between each set.

Variations/progressions

- Use light hand weights instead of Side-Steppers
- Use a 4 or 5 kg jelly ball and work the arms together
- Use punch kick resisters for a lighter resistance

POSITION – GOALKEEPER

DRILL   REACTION BALL

Aim
To develop lightning-quick reactions.

Area/equipment
Outdoor or indoor area but not a grass surface. Use 1 Reaction Ball or a rugby ball.

Description
Work in pairs; the goalkeepers stand 5 yards apart. The ball is thrown so that it lands in front of the goalkeeper, because of the structure of the ball it will bounce in any direction. The goalkeeper has to react and catch the ball before it bounces for a second time.

Key teaching points
- Goalkeeper should work off the balls of the feet and in a slightly crouched position with the hands out ready
- The ball should not be thrown hard – it will do the necessary work itself

Sets and reps
2 set of 20 reps with no recovery between each rep and 1 minute recovery between each set.

Variations/progressions
- Goalkeepers work individually or in pairs by throwing the ball against the wall
- Goalkeepers stand on agility discs while throwing the ball to each other

POSITION – GOALKEEPER
DRILL | *BUNT BAT*

Aim
To develop lightning-quick hand–eye co-ordination.

Area/equipment
Outdoor or indoor area. Use a Bunt Bat and tennis balls or bean bags.

Description
Work in pairs; one of the goalkeepers holds the Bunt Bat. Her partner stands about 3–4 yards away and throws a ball or bean bag, simultaneously calling the colour of the ball on the Bunt Bat. The goalkeeper's task is to fend off the ball/bean bag with the appropriate coloured ball on the Bunt Bat.

Key teaching points
- Start throwing the balls/bean bags slowly and gradually build up the speed
- Goalkeeper should be in a get-set position

Sets and reps
3 sets of 25 reps with 30 seconds recovery between each set.

Variations/progressions
- Use different coloured balls/bean bags – when the ball/bean bag has been thrown, it is to be fended off with the corresponding coloured ball on the Bunt Bat
- The goalkeeper stands on an agility disc while performing the drill

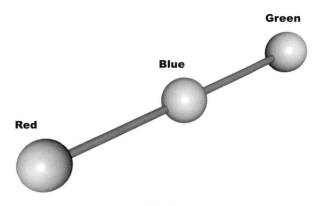

Figure 7.22 Bunt Bat

CHAPTER 8 CORE STABILITY DEVELOPMENT

A core stability ball is not essential to perform functional core stability exercises.

The modern female soccer player needs to be aware of the importance of core control and its impact on performance and injury prevention. By strengthening and toning the lower abdominal muscles (lower transverses) players can accelerate, turn and sprint faster and more safely because there is less impact on the lower back, hamstring and girdle area.

The following exercises will help to develop abdominal strength. Start small then build up to higher reps and sets and more difficult exercises.

The exercises are simple and very functional. They can be performed outdoors or indoors without the need for equipment. Before attempting them, breathe in and out, breathe in again and, holding the contraction, continue breathing while performing the exercise.

DRILL *TIGHT BUTTOCKS*

Aim
To strengthen lower core.

Equipment
None.

Description
Stand up straight with feet a shoulder-width apart. With weight evenly distributed squeeze the buttock muscles (the gluteals) as hard as you can.

Key teaching points
- Keep upright with feet pointing forward
- Do not sink into hips

Sets and reps
Hold for 30 seconds.

DRILL *THE STORK*

Aim
Core stability, proprioception, core balance and control.

Equipment
None.

Description
Stand on one leg and tighten the buttock muscles as hard as possible. Raise one foot as high as comfortably possible and bend the knee at 90°.

Key teaching points
- Keep an upright posture, looking ahead and remaining balanced at all times
- Do not use any supports or sink into hips

Sets and reps
Repeat 25 times on each leg.

DRILL   *LATERAL PELVIC LIFT*

Aim
To develop side core and buttock firmness.

Equipment
None.

Description
Stand on one leg and tighten the buttock muscles as hard as possible, then hold while slightly raising the foot of one leg and lifting the pelvis up.

Key teaching points
■ Keep an upright posture, looking ahead and remaining balanced at all times
■ Do not use any supports or sink into hips

Sets and reps
Repeat 40 times on each leg.

DRILL   *KNEE OUT SQUEEZE*

Aim
To develop core firmness around the hips.

Equipment
None.

Description
Stand on one leg and tighten the buttock muscles as hard as possible. While holding muscles tight raise the knee of one leg out and position the heel of that leg under the groin.

Key teaching points
■ Keep an upright posture and maintain breathing pattern
■ Do not use any supports

Sets and reps
Repeat 40 times on each leg.

DRILL · *BUTTOCK CRUNCHES*

Aim
To develop firm lower core and buttocks.

Equipment
None.

Description
Stand on one leg and tighten the buttock muscles as hard as possible.
While holding muscles tight raise the foot of one leg. Push your raised
leg backwards as you tighten your buttock muscles even harder.

Key teaching points
- Keep an upright posture
- Do not use any supports for balance

Sets and reps
Repeat 25 times on each leg.

DRILL · *STATIC PUSH-UP*

Aim
To develop upper core firmness and control.

Equipment
None.

Description
Get into standard push-up position. Transfer weight equally through
hands and feet. Keep body straight and hold this position.

Key teaching points
- Keep straight body position, holding contraction
- Breathe normally and do not arch back

Sets and reps
Hold position for 25 seconds. Repeat contraction twice.

CHAPTER 9 WARM–DOWN AND RECOVERY

Due to the intense activity levels possible during the main part of the session, time should be given gradually to reduce the heart rate to near resting levels. This will help to:

- Disperse lactic acid

- Prevent blood pooling

- Return the body systems to normal levels

- Assist in recovery

The structure of the warm-down will essentially be the reverse of the Dynamic Flex warm-up, and will last for approximately 5 minutes depending on the fitness level of the players. It begins with moderate Dynamic Flex movements. These will gradually become less intense and smaller in amplitude. These exercises should still focus on quality of movement (good mechanics).

Static stretches should be incorporated following this stage of the session. Perform stretches that mirror the movements that are being carried out in the warm-down.

DRILL *HIGH KNEE-LIFT SKIP*

Follow the instructions given on page 9.

Aim
To warm down the hips and buttocks gradually.

Sets and reps
2 × 20 yards, 1 forwards and 1 backwards.

Intensity
60% for the first 20 yards and 50% for the second 20 yards.

DRILL *KNEE-ACROSS SKIP*

Follow the instructions given on page 10.

Aim
To warm down the hip flexors gradually by lowering the intensity of the exercise.

Sets and reps
2 × 20 yards, 1 forwards and 1 backwards.

Intensity
50% for the first 20 yards and 40% for the second 20 yards.

DRILL *WIDE SKIP*

Follow the instructions given on page 6.

Aim
To warm down the hips and ankles.

Sets and reps
2 × 20 yards, 1 forwards and 1 backwards.

Intensity
40% for the first 20 yards and 30% for the second 20 yards.

DRILL CARIOCA

Follow the instructions given on page 13.

Aim

To warm down the hips and the core.

Sets and reps

2 × 20 yards, l leading with left leg and 1 with right.

Intensity

30% for the first 20 yards and 20% for the second 20 yards.

DRILL SMALL SKIPS

Follow the instructions given on page 5.

Aim

To warm down the muscles of the lower leg and the ankle.

Sets and reps

2 × 20 yards, 1 forwards and 1 backwards.

Intensity

20% for the first 20 yards and 10% for the second 20 yards.

DRILL ANKLE FLICKS

Follow the instructions given on page 4.

Aim

To bring the heart rate down and to stretch the calf and the ankle.

Sets and reps

2 × 20 yards, 1 forwards and 1 backwards.

Intensity

10% for the first 20 yards and then walking flicks for the second 20 yards.

DRILL *HURDLE WALK*

Follow the instructions given on page 18.

Aim
To bring the heart rate down.

Sets and reps
2×20 yards, 1 forwards and 1 backwards.

Intensity
Walking.

DRILL *WALKING HAMSTRING*

Follow the instructions given on page 21.

Aim
To stretch the backs of the thighs.

Sets and reps
2×20 yards, 1 forwards and 1 backwards.

Intensity
Walking.

DRILL   LATISSIMUS DORSI STRETCH

Aim
To stretch the muscles of the back.

Description
Stand in an upright position and link the hands together in front of the chest. Then push the hands out, simultaneously arching the back forwards.

Key teaching points
■ Do not force the arms out too far
■ Focus on slow controlled breathing

Sets and reps
Hold the stretch for about 10 seconds.

DRILL   QUADRICEPS STRETCH

Aim
To stretch and assist the recovery of the thigh muscles.

Description
Stand on one leg and bring the other heel in towards the buttock. Using the hand on that side hold the instep of that foot and squeeze it into the buttock. Repeat on the opposite leg.

Key teaching points
■ Keep the knees together
■ Ensure the support leg is slightly bent
■ Press the hip forward
■ Focus on slow controlled breathing
■ Do not force the stretch, just squeeze it in gently

Sets and reps
Hold the stretch for about 10 seconds on each leg.

Variation
The exercise can be performed while the player is lying down on her side on the floor.

DRILL HAMSTRING STRETCH

Aim
To stretch and assist the recovery of the hamstring.

Description
Work in pairs. One player raises a leg at a 90° angle. The partner holds the back of the heel. The toe of the raised leg is pulled towards the shin (dorsi Flex) and kept straight as the partner gently raises the leg.

Key teaching points
- Focus on slow controlled breathing
- Bend forwards from the hip, do not lean back
- The partner is to assist by raising the leg gently – do not force the stretch

Sets and reps
Hold the stretch for about 10 seconds on each leg.

DRILL ADDUCTORS STRETCH

Aim
To stretch and assist the recovery of the adductor muscles.

Description
Stand with the legs apart, bend one knee and keep the foot at a 45° angle. The other leg should be straight. Repeat on the opposite leg.

Key teaching points
- Focus on slow controlled breathing
- Do not force the stretch
- Keep the back straight
- Do not allow the knee of the bent leg to go beyond the toes

Sets and reps
Hold the stretch for about 10 seconds on each leg.

DRILL CALF STRETCH

Aim
To stretch and assist the recovery of the calf muscles.

Description
Stand with the legs split and both feet pointing forwards, one leg to the front and the other to the back. The weight should be transferred to the forward knee and then gently back. Repeat with other leg.

Key teaching points
- The front knee should not move further than over the ankle
- The back leg should be kept straight – it is this calf that will be stretched
- Focus on slow controlled breathing
- Do not force the stretch
- Apply the weight slowly to the front foot

Sets and reps
Hold the stretch for about 10 seconds on each leg.

The following chapter provides training session and programme samples for both professional and amateur teams, with a focus on pre- and in-season sessions.

The art of any programme is how it is periodised throughout the year plus its ability to accommodate individual needs and variations for unscheduled changes. The best programmes are those which have variety, provide challenges, keep the players on their toes and accept individuality. Too much of the same de-motivates individuals and teams and performance may be compromised.

Some simple rules

■ Start with Dynamic Flex

■ Explosive work and sprints should be completed early in the session before any endurance work

■ Plan sessions so that an explosion session is followed by a preparation day

■ Progress from simple to complex drills

■ Don't restrict programmes to one-week periods, work with different blocks of 4–8–10–12 days

■ Teach one new skill a day

■ Rest and recovery periods to be well planned

■ Vary work-to-rest ratios

■ Build up strength before performing plyometrics

■ Keep session short and sharp. Explanation and discussions should be conducted before and afterwards, not in activity time

■ Finish off session with static (PNF) stretching

Pre–season training

Mention the words 'pre-season training' to most players and you will get a look of horror. For years coaches and trainers have been fixated by the development of the aerobic energy system by utilising long, slow, steady-state runs from 5 miles to anything up to 8 miles. However, research clearly states that this type of activity is not suitable for soccer players but could even make them slower and cause unnecessary injuries.

Most activity in soccer lasts for an average of 5–6 seconds and for about 25 yards in distance. Soccer is a start–stop game, which utilises fast-twitch muscle fibres and primarily depends on the anaerobic system (*see* Glossary, page 170). By training the anaerobic system via explosive drills such as those in this programme, players will benefit in a wide range of ways, including:

■ An increased ability to tolerate higher levels of lactic acid, a by-product of high-intensity activity

■ An increase in aerobic power which is the energy system that uses oxygen without turning off the fast-twitch fibres, vital because it is these that enable soccer players to perform explosive multi-directional movements such as sprinting, jumping, tackling and diving

■ An improved recovery time – this is very important and enables soccer players to perform at a high intensity and to then recover more quickly for the next activity

So it is simple – long, slow runs do not replicate what happens on the field; they are not specific to soccer. Instead, intermittent, intensive runs of various work–rest ratios including sidestep runs, swerves, backward runs and jumps better prepare players for the demands of the game.

The pre-season professional programmes start with a higher percentage of time spent on running mechanics than unexplosive work. As the season draws closer the programme's emphasis progressively changes, with a higher percentage of time being spent on the explosive development and less on the mechanics.

SAQ CONTINUUM	DRILLS	SETS AND REPS	EQUIPMENT	PLAN	TIME
Dynamic Flex	All with ball	Up and back – each drill	Cones and balls	Work in pairs over a 20-yard split grid. Perform a Dynamic Flex drill over the first part of the grid, pick the ball up and perform a ball-skill up and back over the second part of the grid. Return to the start by performing the drill backwards	18 min
Mechanics	▪ Dead-leg run ▪ Lateral step ▪ Single-leg lead Introduce the ball at the end of the grid	1 set of 6 reps of each drill without the ball, and then 1 set of 6 reps with the ball	8 hurdles, cones and balls	Place the hurdles in a straight line with about 18 inches between each hurdle	10 min
Innervation	▪ Single step ▪ Lateral step ▪ Hopscotch ▪ Icky shuffle Introduce the ball in the middle for passing skills	1 set of 6 reps of each drill	4 single ladders, 4 cones and 2 balls	Place the ladders in a cross-formation leaving a space in the middle of about 3 square yards	12 min
Accumulation of potential	A skill circuit incorporating mechanics drills, fast-feet drills and the ball	1 set of 6 reps	12 cones, 2 ladders and 12 hurdles	Place the ladders, hurdles and cones in a circuit to provide the player with the opportunity to practise zigzag, lateral and linear runs forwards and backwards, as well as jump, turn and acceleration mechanics. Incorporate the ball where possible	10 min
Explosion	▪ Out-and-back (include a pass) ▪ Lateral side-stepping ▪ Jockeying with Side-Steppers	1 set of 8 reps of each drill	Viper Belt, Side-Stepper, cones and balls	▪ Out-and-back – wearing a Viper Belt, work out and back to 3 angled cones about 2½ yards away ▪ Zigzag – wearing the Side-Steppers, work in a zigzag pattern along the channel of cones that are about 2 yards apart ▪ Wearing the Side-Steppers, jockey up and back along a 20-yard channel	18 min
Expression of potential	▪ Odd-man-out ▪ British Bulldog	1 game of about 3–4 minutes	Cones and a ball	Split the squad into 4 groups, set up 2 games which can be played simultaneously – after the game, swap the teams around	8 min
Warm-down	Dynamic Flex and static stretching	Up and back – each drill, and 10-second hold on static stretches	Cones	Work over a 20-yard grid for the dynamic flexibility, gradually decreasing the intensity of the drills	12 min

PRE–SEASON PROGRAMME: PROFESSIONAL – WEEK ONE

Tuesday am	Wednesday am	Thursday am	Friday am	Saturday am
Dynamic Flex warm-up 20min	Dynamic Flex warm-up 20min	Dynamic Flex warm-up 20min	Dynamic Flex warm-up 20min	Dynamic Flex warm-up 20min
Mechanics 15min	**Mechanics** 15min	**Mechanics** 15min	**Mechanics** 15min	**Mechanics** 15min
Hurdles, Fast Foot Ladder drills, Dynamic Flex. To develop and perfect the correct linear, lateral and vertical movement mechanics. Increase foot speed and stride frequency				
Soccer Specific Conditioning Innervation 25min	**Soccer Specific Conditioning Innervation** 25min	**Soccer Specific Conditioning Innervation** 25min	**Soccer Specific Conditioning Innervation** 25min	**Competitive Soccer Conditioning** 40min
Soccer related movement drills: Agility, Speed, Multi-direction	Soccer related movement drills: Agility, Speed, Multi-direction	Soccer related movement drills: Agility, Speed, Multi-direction	Soccer related movement drills: Agility, Speed, Multi-direction	Group split into teams. Non-contact competitive soccer movements, drills, games and challenges to increase enjoyment factor. Psychological impact: will increase competitiveness
Explosion	**Explosion**	**Explosion**	**Explosion**	▪ Relays
Resisted, random agility and assisted drills. To develop explosive multi directional speed	Resisted, random agility and assisted drills. To develop explosive multi directional speed	Resisted, random agility and assisted drills. To develop explosive multi directional speed	Resisted, random agility and assisted drills. To develop explosive multi directional speed	▪ Obstacle Courses ▪ Competition Games ▪ Testing
Ratio: Mechanics 70% Explosive 30% Active recovery.	Ratio: Mechanics 70% Explosive 30% Active recovery.	Ratio: Mechanics 70% Explosive 30% Active recovery.	Ratio: Mechanics 60% Explosive 40% Active recovery.	
Soccer Specific Endurance 20min	**Soccer Specific Endurance** 20min	**Soccer Specific Endurance** 20min	**Soccer Specific Endurance** 20min	
Sprint endurance work. e.g. 10×80yd, 8×60yd, 6×40yd Timed active recovery	SAQ Combination runs 3 circuits – timed	Sprint endurance work. e.g. 10×80yd, 8×60yd, 6×40yd Timed active recovery	SAQ Combination runs 3 circuits – timed	
Cool down/	**Cool down/**	**Cool down/**	**Cool down/**	**Cool down/**
PNF Static Stretch 10min	**PNF Static Stretch** 10min	**PNF Static Stretch** 10min	**PNF Static Stretch** 10min	**PNF Static Stretch** 10min
Core stability				Core stability
TOTAL 90min	**TOTAL** 90min	**TOTAL** 90min	**TOTAL** 90min	**TOTAL** 85min
Tuesday pm Football Technical Skills	**Wednesday pm** Football Technical Skills	**Thursday pm** Football Technical Skills	**Friday pm** Football Technical Skills	**Saturday pm** Football Technical Skills

Sunday and Monday

Two-day recovery, personal stretching/swimming

PRE-SEASON PROGRAMME: PROFESSIONAL – WEEK TWO

	Tuesday am	Wednesday am	Thursday am	Friday am	Saturday am
Dynamic Flex warm-up	20min	20min	20min	20min	20min
Mechanics	15min	15min	15min	15min	
Soccer Specific Conditioning **Innervation**	25min Soccer related movement drills: Agility, Speed. Multi-direction	25min Soccer related movement drills: Agility, Speed. Multi-direction	25min Soccer related movement drills: Agility, Speed. Multi-direction	25min Soccer related movement drills: Agility, Speed. Multi-direction	**Competitive Soccer Conditioning** 40min Group split into teams. Non-contact competitive soccer movements, drills, games and challenges to increase enjoyment factor. Psychological impact: will increase competitiveness ■ Relays ■ Obstacle Courses ■ Competition Games ■ Testing
Explosion	Resisted, random agility and assisted drills. To develop explosive multi directional speed	Resisted, random agility and assisted drills. To develop explosive multi directional speed	Resisted, random agility and assisted drills. To develop explosive multi directional speed	Resisted, random agility and assisted drills. To develop explosive multi directional speed	
Ratio:	Mechanics 60% Explosive 40% Active recovery.	Mechanics 60% Explosive 40% Active recovery.	Mechanics 60% Explosive 40% Active recovery.	Mechanics 50% Explosive 50% Active recovery.	
Soccer Specific Endurance	20min Sprint endurance work. e.g. 10×80yd, 8×60yd, 6×40yd	20min SAQ Combination runs 4 circuits – each timed	20min Sprint endurance work. e.g. 11×80yd, 10×60yd, 8×40yd Timed active recovery	20min SAQ Combination runs 4 circuits – timed	
Cool down/ PNF Static Stretch	10min Core stability	10min	10min Core stability	10min	10min Core stability
TOTAL	90min	90min	90min	90min	70min

Tuesday pm	Wednesday pm	Thursday pm	Friday pm	Saturday pm
Football Technical Skills	**Football Technical Skills**	**Football Technical Skills**	**Football Technical Skills**	**Football Technical Skills**

Sunday and Monday

Two-day recovery, personal stretching/swimming

PRE-SEASON PROGRAMME: PROFESSIONAL – WEEK THREE

Tuesday am		Wednesday am		Thursday am		Friday am		Saturday am	
Dynamic Flex warm-up	20min	Dynamic Flex warm-up	20min	Dynamic Flex warm-up	20min	Dynamic Flex warm-up	20min	Dynamic Flex warm-up	20min
Mechanics	15min	Mechanics	15min	Mechanics	15min	Mechanics	15min		
Soccer Specific Conditioning		**Soccer Specific Conditioning**		**Soccer Specific Conditioning**		**Soccer Specific Conditioning**		**Competitive Soccer**	
Innervation	25min	**Innervation**	25min	**Innervation**	25min	**Innervation**	25min	**Conditioning**	40min
Soccer related movement drills: Agility, Speed. Multi-direction		Soccer related movement drills: Agility, Speed. Multi-direction		Soccer related movement drills: Agility, Speed. Multi-direction		Soccer related movement drills: Agility, Speed. Multi-direction		Group split into teams. Non-contact competitive soccer movements, drills, games and challenges to increase	
Explosion		**Explosion**		**Explosion**		**Explosion**		enjoyment factor. Psychological impact: will increase competitiveness	
Resisted, random agility and assisted drills. To develop explosive multi directional speed		Resisted, random agility and assisted drills. To develop explosive multi directional speed		Resisted, random agility and assisted drills. To develop explosive multi directional speed		Resisted, random agility and assisted drills. To develop explosive multi directional speed		■ Relays ■ Obstacle Courses ■ Competition Games ■ Testing	
Ratio: Mechanics 50% Explosive 50% Active recovery.		Ratio: Mechanics 40% Explosive 60% Active recovery.		Ratio: Mechanics 40% Explosive 60% Active recovery.		Ratio: Mechanics 40% Explosive 60% Active recovery.			
Soccer Specific		**Soccer Specific**		**Soccer Specific**		**Soccer Specific**			
Endurance	20min	**Endurance**	20min	**Endurance**	20min	**Endurance**	20min		
Sprint endurance work. e.g. 11×80yd, 10×60yd, 8×40yd		SAQ Combination runs 4 circuits – each timed		Sprint endurance work. e.g. 12×80yd, 10×60yd, 10×40yd Timed active recovery		SAQ Combination runs 4 circuits – timed			
Cool down/		**Cool down/**		**Cool down/**		**Cool down/**		**Cool down/**	
PNF Static Stretch	10min	**PNF Static Stretch**	10min	**PNF Static Stretch**	10min	**PNF Static Stretch**	10min	**PNF Static Stretch**	10min
Core stability				Core stability				Core stability	
TOTAL	90min	TOTAL	90min	TOTAL	90min	TOTAL	90min	TOTAL	70min
Tuesday pm		**Wednesday pm**		**Thursday pm**		**Friday pm**		**Saturday pm**	
Football Technical Skills		Football Technical Skills		Football Technical Skills		Football Technical Skills		Football Technical Skills	

Sunday and Monday

Two-day recovery, personal stretching/swimming

154

PRE–SEASON PROGRAMME: PROFESSIONAL – WEEK FOUR

Tuesday am	Wednesday am	Thursday am	Friday am	Saturday am
Dynamic Flex warm-up 20min	Dynamic Flex warm-up 20min	Dynamic Flex warm-up 20min	Dynamic Flex warm-up 20min	Dynamic Flex warm-up 20min
Mechanics 15min	**Mechanics** 15min	**Mechanics** 15min	**Mechanics** 15min	
Soccer Specific Conditioning **Innervation** 25min Soccer related movement drills: Agility, Speed, Multi-direction	**Soccer Specific Conditioning** **Innervation** 25min Soccer related movement drills: Agility, Speed, Multi-direction	**Soccer Specific Conditioning** **Innervation** 25min Soccer related movement drills: Agility, Speed, Multi-direction	**Soccer Specific Conditioning** **Innervation** 25min Soccer related movement drills: Agility, Speed, Multi-direction	**Competitive Soccer Conditioning** 40min Group split into teams. Non-contact competitive soccer movements, drills, games and challenges to increase enjoyment factor. Psychological impact: will increase competitiveness
Explosion Resisted, random agility and assisted drills. To develop explosive multi directional speed	**Explosion** Resisted, random agility and assisted drills. To develop explosive multi directional speed	**Explosion** Resisted, random agility and assisted drills. To develop explosive multi directional speed	**Explosion** Resisted, random agility and assisted drills. To develop explosive multi directional speed	▪ Relays ▪ Obstacle Courses ▪ Competition Games ▪ Testing
Ratio: Mechanics 30% Explosive 70% Active recovery.	Ratio: Mechanics 30% Explosive 70% Active recovery.	Ratio: Mechanics 30% Explosive 70% Active recovery.	Ratio: Mechanics 30% Explosive 70% Active recovery.	
Soccer Specific **Endurance** 20min Sprint endurance work. e.g. 12×80yd, 10×60yd, 10×40yd Active time recovery reduced	**Soccer Specific** **Endurance** 20min SAQ Combination runs 5 circuits – each timed	**Soccer Specific** **Endurance** 20min Sprint endurance work. e.g. 12×80yd, 12×60yd, 12×40yd Timed active recovery	**Soccer Specific** **Endurance** 20min SAQ Combination runs 5 circuits – timed	
Cool down/ **PNF Static Stretch** 10min Core stability TOTAL 90min	**Cool down/** **PNF Static Stretch** 10min TOTAL 90min	**Cool down/** **PNF Static Stretch** 10min Core stability TOTAL 90min	**Cool down/** **PNF Static Stretch** 10min TOTAL 90min	**Cool down/** **PNF Static Stretch** 10min Core stability TOTAL 70min
Tuesday pm **Football Technical Skills**	**Wednesday pm** **Football Technical Skills**	**Thursday pm** **Football Technical Skills**	**Friday pm** **Football Technical Skills**	**Saturday pm** **Football Technical Skills**

Sunday and Monday

Two-day recovery, personal stretching/swimming

IN–SEASON PROGRAMME: PROFESSIONAL

SATURDAY
OR ONE GAME A WEEK

All sessions start with Dynamic Flex

	A.M.		P.M.	
SUNDAY	Pool recovery, static stretching		Recovery	
MONDAY	**SAQ Session** Resistance work for power Ball work		Strength/power	45 min
TUESDAY	**SAQ Session** Fast feet Mechanics Agility Speed work Ball work		Recovery	
WEDNESDAY	**SAQ Session** Resistance work for power Ball work		Personal circuit conditioning	60 min
THURSDAY	**SAQ Session** Fast feet Mechanics Agility Ball work		Recovery	
FRIDAY	Dynamic Flex		Rest	
SATURDAY	Dynamic Flex, **game**, cool-down		Rejuvenate	

NB: *rest* – feet up and do nothing; *recovery* – active, low-intensity recovery e.g. swimming, walking, stretching, sauna, spa, massage; *rejuvenate* – immediately after game; refuelling and re-hydrating.

IN–SEASON PROGRAMME: PROFESSIONAL

TWO GAMES A WEEK

All sessions start with Dynamic Flex

	A.M.		P.M.	
SUNDAY	Pool recovery		Light ball work Stretching	45 min
MONDAY	Moderate strength/power **SAQ Session** Agility Fast feet Ball work	60 min	Light power	35 min
TUESDAY	Rest Fast feet		**Game**, refuel, recovery	
WEDNESDAY	Rejuvenate		Ball work	
THURSDAY	**SAQ Session** Fast feet Mechanics Agility	45 min	Personal circuit	45 min
FRIDAY	Dynamic Flex Light ball work		Rest	
SATURDAY	Dynamic Flex, **game**, cool-down		Rejuvenate	

Amateur Programme

Amateur teams normally train 2–3 times a week depending on the standard of the leaque they play in. The SAQ Soccer Programme can make training not only interesting and challenging, but also great fun, with the added bonus of good results.

Don't fall into the trap of steady-state runs even at amateur level: interval running and SAQ drills will make your players fitter and faster.

PRE–SEASON PROGRAMME: AMATEUR

1 4 - D A Y   C Y C L E

All sessions start with Dynamic Flex

MONDAY	Start own weight programme and flexibility work	
TUESDAY	Dynamic Flex	15 min
	SAQ Session	40 min
	Interval work:	
	Combination run	5 min (2 min)
	Soccer drills	5 min (2 min)
	Combination run	5 min (2 min)
	Soccer drills	5 min (2 min)
	Combination run	5 min (2 min)
	Soccer drills	5 min (2 min)
	Abdominal work-out, core development stretch	
WEDNESDAY	Active recovery: swimming, stretch	
THURSDAY	Dynamic Flex with ball	15 min
	SAQ Session	40 min
	Power work with jelly balls	
	Interval running	5 min (2 min)
	Soccer drills	5 min (2 min)
	Interval running	5 min (2 min)
	Soccer drills	5 min (2 min)
	Interval running	5 min (2 min)
	Soccer drills	5 min (3 min)
	Stretch, abdominal core development	
FRIDAY	Personal weight-training programme Stretch, swim, sauna	
SATURDAY	Dynamic Flex with ball	15 min
	SAQ Session	
	Power development including recovery	40 min (3 min)
	Soccer drills	40 min (3 min)
	Soccer-specific runs	20 min
	Stretch, swim	
SUNDAY	Stretch – rest	

NB: Time in brackets indicates recovery period before moving on to next element of session.

MONDAY	Start own weight programme, flexibility work	
TUESDAY	Dynamic Flex	15 min
	SAQ Session	40 min
	Interval work:	
	Combination run	5 min (2 min)
	Soccer drills	5 min (2 min)
	Combination run	5 min (2 min)
	Soccer drills	5 min (2 min)
	Combination run	5 min (2 min)
	Soccer drills	5 min (2 min)
	Abdominal work-out, core development, stretch	
WEDNESDAY	Active recovery: swimming, stretch	
	Complex carbohydrate load for Saturday game	
THURSDAY	Dynamic Flex with ball	15 min
	SAQ Session	40 min
	Power work with jelly balls	
	Interval running	5 min (2 min)
	Soccer drills	5 min (2 min)
	Interval running	5 min (2 min)
	Soccer drills	5 min (2 min)
	Interval running	5 min (2 min)
	Soccer drills	5 min (3 min)
	Stretch	
	Complex carbohydrate load for Saturday game	
	Core development	
FRIDAY	Complete rest prior to game, load for Saturday game	
SATURDAY	Dynamic Flex with ball	15 min
	SAQ Session	
	Power development including recovery	40 min (3 min)
	Soccer drills	40 min (3 min)
	Soccer-specific runs	20 min
	Stretch – swim	
SUNDAY	Stretch – rest	

Repeat 14-day programme, reduce recovery times by 20 seconds in the first week and up to 30 seconds in the second week.

NB: Time in brackets indicates recovery period before moving on to next element of session.

IN–SEASON PROGRAMME: AMATEUR

All sessions start with Dynamic Flex

SUNDAY	Rejuvenate/pool recovery	
MONDAY	**SAQ Session** Team ball work Multi-sprints	90 min
TUESDAY	Individual strength and power programme	40 min
WEDNESDAY	**SAQ Session** Team ball work Strength/power work	90 min
THURSDAY	Individual circuit conditioning	40 min
FRIDAY	Warm-up, light ball team-work Rest	75 min
SATURDAY	Warm-up, **game**, cool-down, refuel	

Glossary

Acceleration	Increasing velocity. Specifically over the first 25 yards.
Aerobic	Energy system that uses oxygen.
Agility	The ability to move quickly in any direction and maintain balance.
Anaerobic	Energy system that does not rely on oxygen to function.
ATP	**A**denosine **TriP**hosphate. The only source of energy that muscle can utilise. All food gets broken down into this molecule.
Competitive skills	Skills such as running, jumping or lateral movement that can be used in the sporting environment.
Contrast	A stage after that of resistance where the player/athlete performs the same drill but is unresisted.
Dorsiflexion	Flexing the ankle by lifting the toes, as if one were trying to lift up a bucket with one's toe.
Dynamic	Any movements, particularly those involving stretches, that actively move a limb through its full range of motion.
Explosive	The ability to generate great amounts of force in a very short space of time.
Fast-Twitch fibres	Present in larger proportions in explosive/power athletes, enabling them to perform explosive/powerful movements, as opposed to endurance athletes who possess a greater number of slow-twitch fibres.
Flexibility	Range of motion about a joint. Also the ability of a joint to be elongated.
Force application	Ability to generate the summation of synchronised force to be applied at a specific point in time or space. For example, when throwing a ball.
Goals	An important part of mental preparation in which one thinks about and decides what one wants to achieve.
Hops	Single-leg repeated movements.
Jumps	Double-leg repeated movements.
Lactate	Leftover by-product of anaerobic metabolism that is converted back into ATP by the liver.
Maximum speed	Fastest speed obtainable by an individual, usually achieved between 30 and 50 yards.
Muscular efficiency	The use of stores of muscle energy in a manner that is not wasteful to the athlete, through minimising and eliminating wasted movements.
Neuromuscular recruitment	Activities that work to activate more muscle units.
Peripheral vision	Visual ability to see things or movements while focusing on another object.
Plantar flexion	Pointing the toes downward from the ankle, i.e. full extension of the ankle.

Plyometrics	Any activity that utilises the stretch reflex eliciting rapid changes between eccentric and concentric contractions.	Quicker	To generate a movement in a shorter space of time.
Power output	The rate at which work is done.	Resistance	A type of training that involves tools to increase the force required to move.
Progressive overload	In training, the concept that one needs constantly to force the body to adapt to new stresses.	Specificity	Training precisely for the demands of your sport or skill development.
Proprioception	One's ability to adjust to any stimulus. Can be applied directly to or around the body.	Speed	The ability to move fast over a specific distance.
PNF	Proprioreceptive Neuromuscular Facilitation is a form of training that improves flexibility by increasing the strength of the agonist/primary muscle while decreasing the resistance of the antagonist.	Strength	The raw ability to overcome gravitational or applied forces.

References

Gleim, G.W,. and McHugh, M.P. (1997) 'Flexibility and Its Effects on Sports Injury and Performance', *Sports Medicine*, 24(5): 289–99.

Hennessy, L., Dr (2000) 'Developing Explosive Power', Paper, SAQ Symposium, June 2000.

Pope, R. C. (1999) 'Skip the Warm-up', *New Scientist*, 18 Dec., 164(2214): 23.

Smythe, R. (2000) 'Acts of Agility', *Training and Conditioning*, 5(4): 22–5.

Whall, R. (2000) 'Conditioning the Goalkeeping – a Scientific Approach', Univeristy of Liverpool.

Index of drills

Adductors stretch 147
Agility runs – 4-corner ball 78
Ankle flicks 4, 144
Arm mechanics – buttock bounces 39
   – mirror drills 38
   – partner drills 37

Ball drops 96
British bulldog 104
Buttock crunches 141

Calf stretch 148
Carioca 13, 144
Chair get-ups 85
Circle ball 105
Conditioned games – '2 touch' 108
Cone turns 109

Drop jumps 102

Fast foot ladder – crossover 63
   – giant crossover 69
   – Ipswich town grid 68
   – lateral passing 67
   – long pass 70–71
   – mirror 64
   – single runs 59–61
   – T formation 62
   – with a ball 65
   – with passing 66
Flexi-cord – buggy run 86
   – lateral ball work 88
   – out and back 87
   – overspeed 90
   – vertical power 89

Grid variations 30
Grid variations 32–33

Hamstring buttock flicks 15
Hamstring stretch 147
Hand-weight drops 94
Heel to inside of thigh skip 16
High knee-lift skip 9, 143
Hurdle walk 18, 145

Jumping – multiple jumps 48–49
   – single jumps 47

Knee out skip 7
Knee out squeeze 140
Knee-across skip 10, 143

Lateral pelvic lift 140

Lateral running 11
Latissimus Dorsi stretch 146
Let-goes 84
Line drills 72

Medicine ball (jelly ball) workout 98

Odd one out 107

Pair drill – forward/backward
    run with contact 27
   – jockeying 26
   – lateral runs 25
   – side by side contact run 28
Parachute running 95
Plyometric circuit 101
Plyometrics –low-impact quick jumps 100
Position – all defenders
   – cutting across the opponent 114
   – press and jockey backwards 112
   – pressing a cleared ball 113
Position – attacking midfielders
   – turn and attack 117
Position – centre forward
   – vertical explosive heading power 125
Position – forwards
   – cross and attack goal 124
   – peel off and turn 122
Position – goalkeeper
   – acceleration and jump drill 131
   – bunt bat 137
   – explosive diving 130
   – explosive ground reaction 132
   – explosive hand/arm reaction 135
   – eye-hand reaction 133
   – lateral speed development 129
   – narrowing the angles 127–128
   – peripheral awareness 134
   – reaction ball 136
Position – midfielders
   – assisted/resisted arcing/angled runs
    120
   – backward turn and cover 116
   – ball control, feed, turn, receive, shoot
    118
   – lateral lunges with the ball 119
   – Palmer drill 115
   – overspeed arc running 121
Position – wing back
   – attacking wing back drill 111
Position – winger

– acceleration/deceleration stride drill
    123
Pre-turn 12

Quadriceps stretch 146
Quick box steps 73

Robbing the nest 106
Running form – complex mechanics 56–57
   – curved angle run 55
   – dead-leg run 40
   – hurdle mirror drills 53–54
   – lateral step 45
   – leading leg run 42
   – pre-turn 41
   – quick sidestep development 43
   – sidestep development 44
   – stride frequency and stride length 50
   – with a ball 51–52
   – 1-2-3 lift 46
Russian walk 19

Seated forward get-up 83
Selection of sprints 29
Side lunge 14
Side-stepper – explosive drills 91
   – jockeying in pairs 93
   – resisted lateral runs 92
Sideways heel flicks 17
Single-knee dead-leg lift 8
Sled running 99
Small skips 5, 144
Soccer-specific runs 81
Split grid 31
Static push-up 141
Swerve-development runs 77

The stork 139
Tight buttocks 139
T-runs 75–76

Uphill runs 97

Walking hamstring 21, 145
Walking lunge 20
Walking on the balls of the feet 3
Wall drill – knee across body 24
   – leg out and across body 22
   – linear leg forward/back 23
W-drills 79
Wide skip 6, 143

Zigzag runs 80